If Only I Could Tell Them

by
ZAK

Olympus Story House

Contents

PREFACE

My face is adorable, my body is soft
My disposition is an even temperament... extremely affectionate
My loyalty to Mr. & Mrs. Bonzo is unshakable
They're my Mother and Father, providers of love, grooming,
food and cookies
P.S. They have encouraged my wanderlust
(We travel extensively)

Now you may not think an adorable little guy like me has much to say.

Bonzos tell me everyday that I am so special and I can do anything just try.

So, I said to myself one day, I too have a book to write, Mrs. Bonzo says there is a story in all of us she is great!!!

To some of you readers, I may not be a Gunga Din, Alexander the Great or Eisenstein

For a Soft Coated Wheaton Terrier, Elbe Bonzos think I am one outstanding little fella.

You see, to them I am their son we are a team of three, we are inseparable.

My life has been exciting, interesting and I hear the Bonzos say We've just begun. So before we continue on our lives journey,

I thought I had better put in writing the events I have experienced thus far.

Don't be harsh on my first publication, it's an effort of love and devotion to the Bonzos, the two most wonderful people in my life,

I'll admit completely dysfunctional, but that's part of their charm.

My mission is to make you smile, feel love and understand my life as I see it!

ZAK

Chapter 1

AM I A CUTE PUPPY

It is hard to remember everything, we all have selective memories, the good, the bad, somehow many fade into the distance, and yet there are some memories that will always remain precious. Ibis story is about the life I have led in the company of two people whose escapades could probably give folklore a bad name. They have adored me, made me happy and in their company I seemed to flourish, I hope they see themselves as I see them.

It all started so long ago, as a puppy even to myself I seemed small in stature, and although I sported light and dark brown markings all over me, I resembled all the other small puppies in the litter. I came from a pet store... well not really, I actually came from Iowa. I was born on January 3rd, at kennels in the middle of nowhere and in the depths of winter, in a place such as Iowa which is not the sun worshipped playground of the rich and famous, life started for me so bleak and desolate.

I can't remember very much about my first few weeks, but I do remernber a lot of feeding, and trying to walk, which in my case proved somewhat difficult, in the midst of several other puppies all trying to get lunch or dinner. For those of you familiar with the sight of hungry puppies walking over one another, you may think it is endearing, but if you were like me, in the middle of the pack, it was like a linebackers meeting in an NFL game.

After a couple of months, of pretty much doing the same thing every day, there came that day that was to change my life. Some of us, young puppies were herded into a truck in small pint sized cages, off on what I thought might be a great adventure. I could not have known what was to await me.

ZAK

Journey seemed endless, and not much of an adventure, mostly bouncing up and down, is this how life is, full of ups and downs? Such is the plight of young puppies, at such an early age facing the unknown. Where would I find my self situated.

When you are in the dark, in the back of a truck it can be very intimidating, how can you know where life will lead you. The truck stopped quite a few times, but gathered speed each time, swaying and rattling, my heart sank at the thought of more of this, I fell asleep, hoping to wake up in Disneyland, or at the very least in an environment with lots of bones, treats, and bottled water, preferably French.

When I did wake up, the truck was not moving, puppies were whimpering, and I looked through the crack in the side of the truck and could see bright sunshine. Cages started to move out of the truck, was I about to leave?

I was hoisted in the air, my cage rattling, and with my heart in my mouth, I closed my eyes and took a deep breath. I opened one eye, slowly, and found myself in a strange world of puppies, pussy cats, and birds, strange noises filled the air. Where am I? I pondered over and over again, where am I?

Where I found myself was in a pet store in Newport Beach, California, such a long way from Iowa.

"Sign here lady" said a large strange looking animal, and another strange looking one, counted all the puppies. Both are strangely reminiscent of animals I saw where I was born, two legged variety and for someone my size, extremely tall.

I was taken from my cage and put in another one, only this was a little larger than I was used to, just a little. There was lots of paper on the bottom of my cage, and a bowl with water, unfortunately tap water. I was ten weeks old, so my first thought is where do I follow nature's way of feeding, there is no mother puppy.

The cage door opened and another puppy entered into what I thought was a place to call mine, and mine alone. This animal was much bigger than me, and growled. It bumped into me, all so terribly annoying. I had no idea who this infernal four legged variety was, but he has an odor to which I was not particularly partial.

2

IF ONLY I COULD TELL THEM

I sat down, I had found so far in my young life, and still do, when you have a problem one of the best things to do is sit, and think it through, it also helps if you have a bewildered look on your face. At that moment I did.

Days went by it seemed like an eternity, and I was still in this awful cage, the two-legged variety of tall people, that I had now got used to, passed by it was an endless stream. They had funny looks on their faces, and kept saying things like "Oh what a cute puppy", "Look at that cute puppy" over and over again, "Daddy, Daddy, look at the cute puppy" vocalized by smaller versions of the tall people. I have surmised at this point, and you, the reader, may have questioned this, what breed am I? Well, after much deliberation I decided it's obvious, I am a Cute.

Now you may never have heard of this breed before, but I assure you many puppies come under the cute breed. I was taken out of the cage petted, put back, taken out again, it really was quite boring. After a few days I was getting sick and tired of being told I am a cute puppy, but at least I knew what I was.

Sometimes, passers by, would ask one another, what breed they thought I could be. I felt like shouting were I able, "Cute, of course you idiots" but I stayed quietly aloof. If they don't know, who am I to tell them.

Then one day, just six days after I arrived, a handler stuck his hand in my cage, pulled me out, and put me in the arms of a gentleman, not particularly distinguished, and sporting spectacles.

I snuggled into him, and almost immediately he was joined by an elegant, sophisticated lady, apparently the two were together, somehow they seemed an odd couple. She petted me, "Oh what a cute puppy" she said. I shall refer to these two from here on as Mr. and Mrs. Bonzo simply because it's always fun to come up with names for humans.

"What is it?" says Mrs. Bonzo, "A Soft Coated Wheaton Terrier", replied Mr. Bonzo.

I was stunned, whatever is a Soft Coated Wheaton Terrier, it's not me I am a Cute.

Days went by it seemed like an eternity, and I was still in this awful cage, the two-legged variety of tall people, that I had now got

3

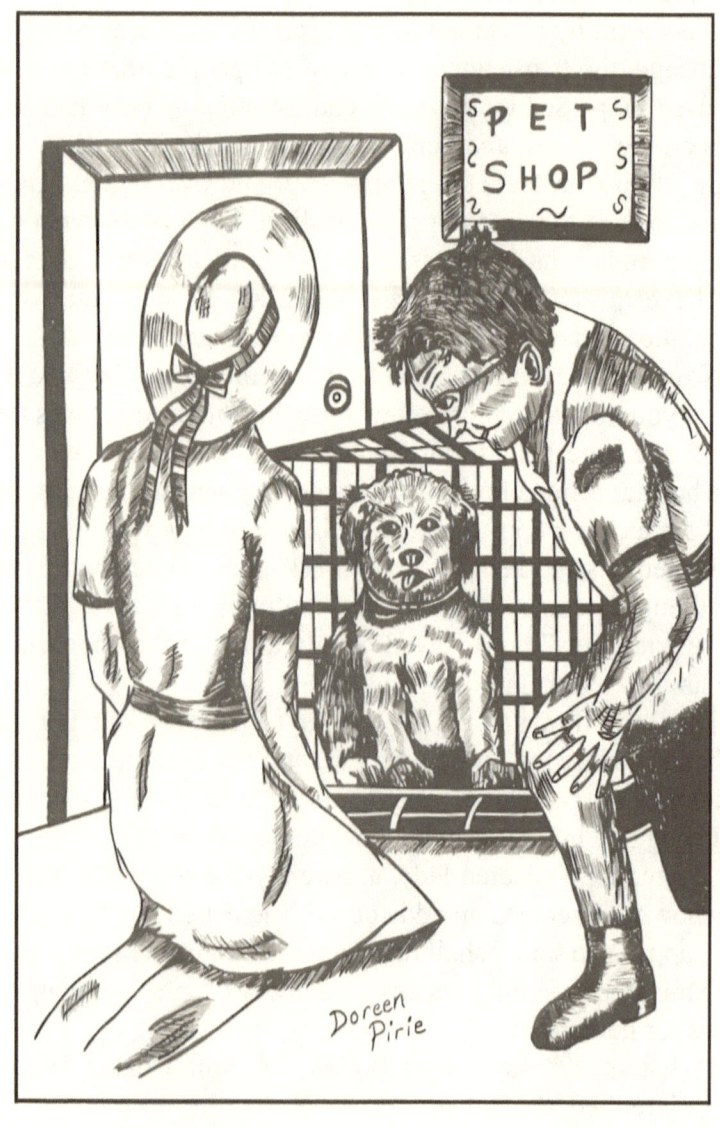

used to, passed by it was an endless stream. They had funny looks on their faces, and kept saying things like "Oh what a cute puppy", "Look at that cute puppy" over and over again, "Daddy, Daddy, look at the cute puppy" vocalized by smaller versions of the tall people. I have surmised at this point, and you, the reader, may have questioned this, what breed am I? Well, after much deliberation I decided it's obvious, I am a Cute.

Now you may never have heard of this breed before, but I assure you many puppies come under the cute breed. I was taken out of the cage petted, put back, taken out again, it really was quite boring. After a few days I was getting sick and tired of being told I am a cute puppy, but at least I knew what I was.

Sometimes, passers by, would ask one another, what breed they thought I could be. I felt like shouting were I able, "Cute, of course you idiots" but I stayed quietly aloof. If they don't know, who am I to tell them.

Then one day, just six days after I arrived, a handler stuck his hand in my cage, pulled me out, and put me in the arms of a gentleman, not particularly distinguished, and sporting spectacles.

I snuggled into him, and almost immediately he was joined by an elegant, sophisticated lady, apparently the two were together, somehow they seemed an odd couple. She petted me, "Oh what a cute puppy" she said. I shall refer to these two from here on as Mr. and Mrs. Bonzo simply because it's always fun to come up with names for humans.

"What is it?" says Mrs. Bonzo, "A Soft Coated Wheaton Terrier", replied Mr. Bonzo.

I was stunned, whatever is a Soft Coated Wheaton Terrier, it's not me I am a Cute.

"Oh he's darling" Mrs. Bonzo, lovingly approves.

"Are we getting him?" she asked.

Mr. Bonzo didn't look too sure, but I was cuddled up against him, and up to now these two appeared to be my best bet to get out of the cage forever, so I thought I might work my charm on them. It was St. Patrick's Day, and how much more appropriate can it be, to take home a wheaten puppy, on St. Patrick's Day since wheaten's originated in Ireland. Cute's apparently originated in Iowa.

5

I sniffed them, as puppies can do appearing as though it was a loving kiss, and licked them both on the cheek, but just as I thought it was time to return to my cage, the Bonzos looked at each other and to my surprise declared "Lets take him home.

I didn't know whether to be pleased or anxious, as the store owner took me from them, and led me behind closed doors, leaving Mr. Bonzo behind to sign the forms necessary for my departure. Mrs. Bonzo had a broad smile on her face, I had a broad perplexed look about me.

I experienced my first bath, which is more than can be said for my cage mate, still carrying the odor with which he arrived. A handler bathed me all over with shampoo and tepid water, and promptly dried me off, and quickly put me in a small carrying cage.

So much for a long leisurely shower, with expensive perfumed soap, it seemed this was the signal however that I was ready to go. Mr. and Mrs. Bonzo picked me up and proudly announce to one another, at last they have a wheaten. I gathered for some time they have been contemplating owning one, we will just have to see how happy we might be with one another, and if they will always think I am cute.

Chapter 2

DON'T TRY THIS AT HOME

We arrived at their house, and they with great pomp and ceremony they presented me to the living room, bedrooms and other parts of the house as if I should know which room is which. Frankly at my age and current status of apprehension, they all looked alike, and I can't say I was terribly impressed, I had been uprooted once again, bathed, transported in the back of a car, and clearly expected to know my place in this new environment, too much for one day and what's more I was shadowed on every movement. I was too tired to explore or even do puppy things, it was a long day, and tomorrow is another.

Mr. and Mrs Bonzo are somewhat mature, at least in age, She hails from Connecticut, he from Merry Old England. have been together for many years, and as Mr. Bonzo likes to put it, after so many happy years... they met.

Mrs. Bonzo is a graceful and charming lady, with the looks of someone who has been pampered, while he could remind anyone of an English Mr. Magoo, or Inspector Clouseau. I would get to know them in time and not change my opinion.

Staying with them, is a slightly built lady, Mrs. Bonzo's mother, named Frances. She arrived recently form Connecticut, for a short stay, and had no idea that my potty training, was to be left to her devices, and under her authority.

It was early the following morning after my triumphant arrival, that I had my first taste of what I was going to have to experience, "Be a good boy, do your business outside" as I was pooping on the living room carpet. What on earth does that mean, be a good boy? They obviously didn't know I was too young to understand a word they were saying, I think I am pretty good, at least by puppy standards, however Mrs Bonzo, went into fits of "Naughty boy" and kept pointing at the glass sliding doors in the living room, which I can't say I am totally in love with, since on the day of my arrival my nose had on a number of occasions met with them usually at several miles per hour.

Frances on the other hand had, a different approach, she would pick me up and leave me in the garden, as if I would know what to do, and where to do it, why is it humans expect puppies to be on the same wavelength as they are? Often she would point her finger at me, advising of the dangers of not responding to this action. What is it with people from Connecticut, constantly finger pointing, it must have something to do with the cold winters.

I was eating quite well, which probably accounts for the activity at my rear end, and the water tasted good, and delightfully bottled French, but I just can't help it, when I have to go, I have to go. The trick was to go, when they are not looking, run away, and hide.

This has not been very successful for me so far, on account that I have no camouflage. Their carpet is a light colored cream, and their furniture matches my coloring, at least for the time being. There also doesn't seem to be too many hiding places, but I haven't explored everywhere yet, in time I will. All day I seemed to be under supervision, it was like boot camp.

I suppose the Coup De Gras has to be when I went out into the garden for a quiet stroll, and perhaps eat a flower or two, when nature took it's course. Since I was out there in the garden, it seemed appropriate to just do it.

I could not have imagined in my wildest dreams, what was to follow. After my brief event, the whole two-legged entourage from the house appeared, whooping and cheering and wildly applauding. "Good Boy," they kept repeating "Wonderful, wonderful." I believe they thought I was trained, they couldn't understand at that time I was an Untrained Pupfessional.

For those not familiar with the "Shofar" it is a ram's horn, used for centuries in the Middle East and around the world, for various reasons, for example to warn of an enemy approach, to greet strangers greet strangers and so on. In the Synagogue it is blown to welcome in the Jewish New Year and also to end the Day of Atonement, mostly by those who know how to blow it.

Mr. Bonzo has not as yet perfected the art, but as I crept through the sliding doors amid the ecstasy that surrounded the moment, a shrill long blast from the Shofar erupted, not particularly well struck, I may add, whereupon with impeccable timing, and based on sheer panic I pooped on the living room carpet. At that moment all Shofar blowing stopped, and I ran for cover.

Oh no I thought here comes the finger waving, but everyone was standing motionless in silence, including a silent Shofar. It was as if someone had died, or all there was a power outage, and there was no sound from the television, terribly frightening for a young puppy, in the early stages of getting frisky after a successful poop.

I was getting the impression, they want me to go outside, but I thought I will still give them fits, by looking like I am going in the house, turning in ever decreasing circles like whirling dervish. Having tried this, I can tell you, all that happened was I got picked up like a rag doll and shunted into the yard.

Perhaps it is best I just follow instructions, and my advice to puppies everywhere is, don't try my method at home if you are an untrained pupfessional.

Chapter 3

THE LEASH

Up to now I have had the pleasure or should I say freedom to roam around at will, wherever I choose. Explore the accommodations in which I have it seems secured a home, wander into the garden and generally feel at ease with my abode, Mr. Bonzo apparently has other ideas for me. An Englishman by birth, an American in spirit, he would speak in the style of his native tongue, and has little time for stupidity except of course his own.

I had not really noticed that I have a collar around my neck, until a leash was placed on it, and a restriction on my hitherto unfettered existence. Now suddenly I was expected to tag along at his pleasure, go where he wanted to, and at a pace that suits him.

It all started with a "Shall we go for a walk, Zak" spoken with a soft voice and reminiscent of the kind of romantic tone afforded ladies in wide brim hats, and Victorian gowns, parading along a coastal shore, on a balmy summer evening. I stood my ground as I felt a little pull on my collar, with Mr. Bonzo heading toward the front door. I was still in the living room, where frankly I intended to remain.

"Come on Zak" the voice a little stronger now "Walkies." I decided not to budge, after all I was not used to being told where I was going to go. "Zak, I said Walkies" the voice gaining decibels, and the tone lifting from Tenor to Alto Soprano. I stared, hoping to look bemused, or even put on my bewildered face, but the tugging on my collar was getting a little ferocious by now, and that started to irritate me.

10

No I thought, Wheatens can be stubborn, according to the AKC and most books you can read on dog training, and besides my lot originated in Ireland, which affords me the luxury.

His pulling got worse, he was halfway out the front door, and I was still in the living room. I am winning I thought, as the delivery of instructions reached a crescendo that, most operatic sopranos could muster. With me barking and him pulling, I was surprised to see him disappear out the front door as it unexpectedly closed with a bang.

Now this was an interesting turn of events, since I couldn't see him, and also couldn't move, and he was now using language I had not heard before.

Although it doesn't take much of an imagination, to visualize a

middle age man with a dog leash stuck in the framework of a thick door shouting and screaming, I was not able to see what passers by and the neighborhood generally could witness and many did.

Unfortunately, as the door closed it locked, and my master, did not have a key at his disposal! I wonder whom you call under such circumstances, a locksmith, AAA, dog side assistance. Lucky for him Mrs. Bonzo appeared, returning from her weekly trip to the beauty parlor. As she approached to drive into the garage, wails of laughter could be heard coming from her, and probably heard as far as the next area code. She let him in, despite possible interference with a session of redoing whatever has already been done to her hair. Normally this is a half hour ritual, with which neither man nor beast must interfere.

With the door now open, me comfortably situated in a fine sit- ting position, in the living room, Mr. Bonzo entered. Unlike the Shofar blowing incident, this was not a silent moment. If you have wondered what the noise must be like when they run the bulls in Pamplona, you might consider the rage of a tormented Englishman as probably equal.

As the raging bull approached me, he swooped me up in his arms, carried me out of the now unlocked front door, and placed me on the kerb, naturally I sat down. The Englishman calmer than before, said "Now Zak, we are going for a walk" I mentally made

11

note, in the future never to respond to what we are going to do. On the bright side, I was out in the street, there is grass on the sidewalk, the sun is shining, and lots of things happening out here. There are people, large funny looking things moving very fast, I wonder if they are relatives of mine, since they have four wheels, and of course I have four legs. Illey might be big cousins.

"Zak don't go near the cars" shouted Mr. Bonzo, as a Volkswagen goes by, or is it a German Shepherd. I suppose a Maserati is the equal of an Italian Greyhound, Toyota equals an Akita and any American SUV is equivalent to a sheepdog, since it can herd families of four over rugged terrain called local mall parking lots, awash with speed bumps. I think I know why Sharpeis walk slowly, Orientals drive at 25 mph even on highways.

By the way I was still sitting on the sidewalk, there had been no movement on my part, a little tugging, from whence this comes should be no surprise, and a small gathering of neighbors eager to see our continuing battle. Mr. Bonzo explains to the assembly, that this is my first time on a leash, I made another mental note, watch out for any sign, that suggests, first time for anything.

In the kind of accent that would grace the London stage, and speech pattern that would make Shakespeare proud, Mr. Bonzo states, it seems convincingly, not so to me, he knows how to train a dog. By virtue of his demeanor, all that was missing, was for him to be attired in khaki shorts and a pith helmet, we shall see if he knows how to train a dog, in my view, stubborn is the stance to take. Yet another tug of war ensued as he pulled frantically on the leash, and I took a firm stance, back legs rooted to the ground, at a forty five degree angle, and my head about three feet in advance of my body, I was not ready for stretching, or to become a Dachshund, the long sausage type dog with very little legs all at different angles.

At that very moment, I thought I was winning, my back legs caved in, and at my age who would blame them, as I was dragged forward.

"See" exalts Mr. "Nothing to it," as my behind goes dragging and sagging forward at a snails pace.

"You've just got to be firm," declares a now smiling Englishman. The gathered assembly are neither amused nor convinced; believing

they have just seen the local Mr. Magoo in action as they wander off to parts unknown. We limped along another few yards, when Mr. Bonzo turned to make his way back to the front door, me in tow, still dragging and sagging. After much deliberation I am convinced we "walked" all of six yards.
Proudly, heads held high we enter the house.

"Back so soon" says Mrs. Bonzo, and an interested Frances, who perhaps had ideas of grandeur she would parade me on jaunts along the tree lined avenues.

"Yes dear, and a very promising start to training him," declared Mr. Bonzo.

The leash came off, and I was free again, free to roam the house and garden, get some water from my bowl, do anything I want, like play with my toys, ah yes, life can all right if you take the line of leash resistance.

Chapter 4

A TRIP TO THE VET

Mr. Bonzo was gazing at me as I sat in the kitchen, pondering about life in general, and the possibility of a treat from a kitchen cupboard. I have become used to sitting, and for the most part staring at the cupboard in the corner of the kitchen in the hope someone will pay attention to my need for a dog cookie, or a treat purchased at the pet store, or even Beluga caviar.

On that occasion, Mr. Bonzo momentarily disappeared, before returning and waving the infernal leash at me, with a statement that quite frankly shocked me. "Zak" he started, "We are going to the vet, so you can get your shots." I have familiarized myself with some words or phrases they keep repeating, but shots was not something I had heard before. What shots, does he mean, a shot and a beer, target practice, what does he mean vet?

I was unceremoniously bundled in to the car, my leash attached by now, and placed onto a towel I recognize from my early pee anywhere days, and as if by nature I lay flat on the back seat, not on the towel. "Zak, lie on the towel please" Mr. Bonzo declares "We can't have you on the seat, lie on the towel" I am sure he doesn't remember I peed on this once.

We got underway, my rear end bouncingup and down, which certainly makes it difficult to peer out of the window, and my head nodding like little stuffed animals you see in the back window of the cars. It seems to me we are on the journey, but where are we going? Mr, Bonzo is listening to his radio, the sun is shining, tress are passing by at enormous speeds, and my rear end continuously bouncing. It didn't take long before we came to a stop outside of a building, from which I could hear barking and strange noises I experienced from different animals, while up for sale at the pet store.

"Here we are Zak" Mr. Bonzo stated the obvious, "Come on little one, we are going to see the vet."

As I entered through the front doors, I was overcome with two thoughts. First there are other dogs in here, they are sitting and waiting patiently, although some are wrestling with their owners in a kind of tug of war game, and the place itself looks interesting. On the hand, I am here for something called shots, and that might take away the joy of the company of other four-legged animals. Then there are the smells, those coming from our very own four-legged variety, and a distinct odor that I have not smelled before, it seems antiseptic in nature.

Mr. Bonzo picked me up and carried me to a counter; where there are a number of ladies all dressed similarly in a long blue nylon coats. Couldn't they have called each other, to see who was wearing what, that morning?

"Good morning" said one young lady, smiling at me, "Who do we have here." I wish I could have said Mr. Bonzo, but alas I was and am still not a dog prodigy able to communicate to humans in their native tongue.

"This is Zak," explained the Englishman.

"Oh isn't he cute" said the nylon blue coat, and still looking at me uttered.

"Do we have an appointment"?

Once again I was hoping to butt in with, "No we just came in for a cup of coffee and a doggie treat, and by the way are you doing anything tonight," but as I explained verbal communication is a problem.

Mr. Bonzo went into his we are here for his shots routine, and yes we have an appointment.

"Just wait a few minutes and the Doctor will be with you," said the young lady, repeating once gain how cute I am.

"Lady I am a soft coated Wheaton terrier, not a cute" I said, well not said, actually I barked, but the sentiment was in there somewhere.

16

While sitting and behaving myself, a strange occurrence in my short lifetime, I couldn't help noticing, other dogs came in different shapes and sizes. I was trying to figure out who was what, when most of the people there did it for me.

Isn't it strange, gathering a group of people together all with their own dogs, and if not already, prospective dog lovers, yet, the first thing they say to another person with a dog is "What kind of dog is that?"

You would think they would know. Before long the crowd is in raptures when they find, this one is a Golden Retriever, that one is a Hungarian Puli. Of course everyone had to ask Mr. Bonzo what breed was I, and so I keep on wondering why is this so hard for people to mistake me for a Cute, even though Mr. Bonzo is wearing a tee shirt with a graphic of a Wheaten Terrier clearly displayed an name of my breed written underneath in letters so large anyone wit pathetic vision could identify the text.

When asked what I was, he sarcastically replied to a lady comforting a small toy poodle, and who seemed only slightly interested that she would get a response to her question, "He's a Nepalese Yak Hunter, we had him specially imported from the upper slopes of the Himalayas." he stated. Ilis satisfied it would seem, and ended any further discussion.

In the waiting room, there is a notice board which among other items includes a lost and found section with photographs of other furry creatures.

How do they get lost, I wondered and for a brief moment it occurred to me that I might be lost. Further inspection of the board reminded me I was not.

'Large Terrier found at the corner of First and Main, answers to the name of Jack' probably his real name is Butch, but whoever found him called him Jack.

'Siamese Cat seen wandering outside Buddhist Temple' for it's twin seemed confusing, since it was lost, how could it find it's twin.

'Has anyone seen our dog Candy' the notice read with a Polaroid photograph of a small white poodle, ' Last seen panhandling outside the jewelers in the High Street, important we find her. This was just above a police notice that contained a report of a robbery in the area. The suspect described as short, white and very disheveled, about two feet in height "Possibly wearing a mask over her head."

I hope I never appear on the board, although I might post myself one day ' Loving Adorable Soft Coated Wheaten Terrier, tremely intelligent, with a sense of humor, loves walks on the beach romantic dinners sharing one bowl, classical music and adventures in prickly hedges, seeks single Wheaten female with similar interests.

After a few minutes young blue coat called to Mr. Bonzo and me, and motioned toward a door, "The Doctor will be with you shortly." Mr. Bonzo muttered "Sure, sure.

We entered a small room, with a long bench, a small counter on to which I was hoisted, and a small weighing machine. I sat on the counter, at seemingly a great height. I have never been up in this rarified air before.

I looked at the Englishman, wondering what is going to happen to me next. It seemed, as though nothing much was going to happen when another blue coat arrived and put me on a weighing machine. "Eleven and a half pounds" she pronounced, "He's a growing boy."

She was on her way out when she looked at Mr. Bonzo and said, Doctor will be with you shortly."

Mr. Bonzo apparently has had experiences waiting for doctors, dentists, and many other professionals in the past, so it was no surprise his response had a taste of sarcasm to it.

"Why" retorted Mr. Bonzo "Has there been a sighting of him?"

He turned toward me and muttered "Zak there's as much chance of seeing a Yeti, ...shortly."

Sometimes when waiting, it can seem longer than it really is, but let's say it seems like five minutes when it is only a minute. Does that mean for a dog, you would multiply by seven automatically and therefore it seems like thirty-five minutes.

The Doctor appeared, and presented himself, "I'm Randy" he said, well aren't we all I thought.

He proceeded to examine me, touching places nobody had before, my ears, heart, nose, and after a minute or two pronounced me healthy. This was apparently good news for Mr. Bonzo, who looked at me, and rubbed my head. He had done this before, as a sign of affection, but not in public, I thought it embarrassing.

"Now, for the shots" exclaimed the vet, and without me even seeing it, a needle was inserted somewhere near my rear end was followed by a strange sensation as he put some sort of capsule near my nose and squeezed, the capsule that is, not my nose. Wow, I pondered, don't people get arrested for sniffing stuff like this?

This brief medicinal event over, the vet offered me a small treat. I looked at it carefully, this was not my normal treat, it smelled differently and frankly was a lot smaller than I was used to, but I ate it, and decided I prefer home treats. Mr. Bonzo went into raptures about how well behaved I had been, and the vet concurred.

"How big do you think he will grow?" questioned Mr. Bonzo.

"He has big paws, and I should think about thirty five to forty pounds," answered the Randy man.

"Really, that big" said a frowned looking Mr. Bonzo.

He has big paws, and I should think about thirty five to forty pounds, answered the Randy man.

"Really that big" said the frowned Mr. Bonzo

At this point it got me concerned too. If I am to grow to that sort of size, how will I be able to hide behind the sofa, or in case of need, some small corner of the house when I want a little peace and quiet?

What if at that size I am no longer cute, at the present time I can run through the garden turn on a dime, chase birds, evade the sprinklers or take a shower in them when I feel like it, will I be able to do all that when I am bigger? Will I have to go on a diet, will they still love me?

Mr. Bonzo has nnore questions, "When will he pee with his leg up?"

Not only was Randy taken aback with this question, but also so was I. Pee with my leg up !!! I am peeing perfectly well thank you, squatting, changing my ablution habits are not on my agenda.

"He may never," replies a startled Randy. I barked, intending the following sentiment "Gentlemen discussing the bathroom habits

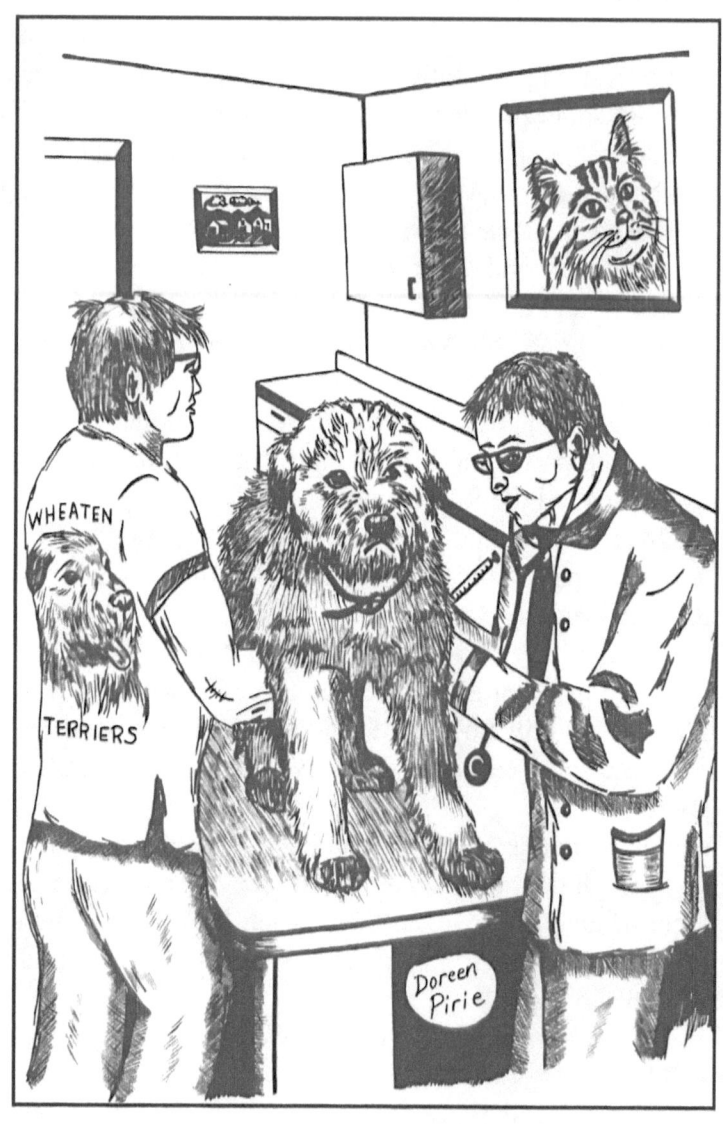

of a Wheaten Terrier is a subject I can live without. What if asked either of you how it felt standing up at the toilet, or how would you pee with your leg up.

Question time over we say our goodbyes and as they shook hands, I was left bewildered at the whole event.

I began to feel a little sleepy, as I was put on the floor and paraded in front of the counter again.

Blue coat was still there, "Would you like to set up his next appointment," she said to Mr. Bonzo. Another appointment I thought does this mean I am going to have to go through his again.

"Yes" was the reply I didn't want to hear.

With that done, we left the doggie smells behind, the antiseptic aroma, and the blue coat brigade, and headed for the car. "Good boy Zak" beams Mr. Bonzo, "We are going home."

So, my first visit to the vet was over, I was rear ended, sniffed something or other, got a treat I didn't like, was fussed over by blue coats, and found out I am going to be huge, and suffered the indignity of what I can only call the "Rear, Nose and Throat Department.

Chapter 5

MY FIRST REAL OUTING

Not for the first time I was awakened from a short nap. I like taking a nap once in a while, usually on the kitchen floor which I like, it is cool, and slippery, when Mr. And Mrs. Bonzo are not around I can pretend I am ice skating, although I have not perfected the triple axel or attempted a quad, but that also means I won't have Judges collaborating over me in the Doggie Olympics, as to whether I finished last or one from last.

Shiny floor skating usually occurs when I need a drink of water, and at full speed enter the arena from the garden put the brakes on and come to a screeching halt at the water bowl. Sometimes my steering is not what it should be, and I would hit the bowl containing my food, which could splatter everywhere. "Muse are times I quickly eat it up from different parts of the kitchen, so no one will notice.

Today however it seems we are off again in the car, Mrs. Bonzo is coming with us. I heard the hall closet door open and close which means the leash must be coming out, so I quickly skated across floor make for the living room and try and hide.

"Zak, where are you" I hear, "Peoria, Illinois" is the kind of reply I would like to give them, using my best Irish brogue. It really doesn't help to try and evade them, in the end they always find me and always manage to lead me to wherever they want to go. Before long I am bouncing around on the back seat of the car, which always became tedious. have seats for children why not dog seats, if I could have one, it would save my behind a lot of trouble, and most probably my sanity. We arrived at our destination, which to my surprise is where I first landed in Southern California, Newport Beach. I was pleased to get out of the car, but now they were trying to make me walk on a leash again. I would let them think I have finally got the hang of it.

They say you can't go home again, as we stroll around Fashion Island, we approach the Pet Store, where my first taste of a new life began, where if memory serves me right, there should be a large, smelly ugly dog, in a cage and as yet not taken away by even larger two legged people thinking he's cute. We entered, the place was crowded with people gawking at the puppies, do they know what they look like from inside the cage?

I cannot see anyone I recognize, I wonder if they found homes.

The Bonzos wandered among the shelves looking for treats I was pleased to say, and toys. Whoopee I thought this is good day. I was shown an array of stuffed animals, rubber bones and cookies. I'll take them all I thought. The Bonzos gathered a few things together an departed. It was pleasant to visit the old neighborhood.

Fashion Island is a large open-air upscale mall. There are lots of people around mostly large, not so upscale and all of them seem want to say hello to me. All of them I put in the same category as the crowd at the Vet, "What breed of dog is that?" they always asked. I had now perfected my bark to respond in the hope it sounded like "Nepalese Yak Hunter."

Mrs. Bonzo decided she is going into a department store, and suggested Ms. Bonzo waits for her. I was shocked to find I was not allowed into department stores, surely that is discrimination. Humans take up much more space than puppies; we would not be an encumbrance.

As Mrs. Bonzo disappeared into the store, I was troubled. Here I was in the open-air mall, what if I want to poop. There was no living room carpet here, and as for peeing, with my leg up or not, no place I can see that resembles the garden. To cap it all, there were lots and lots of people around, I have enough trouble with Mr. And Mrs. Bonzo watching me, now shoppers in their upscale hordes would watch. I can't help feeling there must be somewhere for puppies to go, or is this more discrimination. I bet there were restrooms in the department store for humans.

As I pondered the thoughts of the day, I couldn't help prevent the urge to go, intending not to worry any more on the subject, I started my now famous whirling dervish routine, rotating at high speed, which Mr. Bonzo noticed with some dismay, since this signaled the need to go.

He tugged at my leash and started to walk to a secluded corner, I continued round and round in ever decreasing circles. I should advise the reader at this point, that although I had gained weight I was not yet at the point of being strong enough to combat Mr. Magoo. Just wait until I am thirty-five or forty pounds, I thought to myself, we'll see who wins then.

As we approach the place he selected I could see the ocean in the distance, but my view was interrupted as he pushed me behind a bush, with the probable expectation that no one could see me, and I would be pleased to oblige instantaneously It's not that easy, to go on command, particularly without the right preparation, a few smells, eat some grass, select a decent spot of my own, that I feel comfortable with, and make sure I leave a trail of thoroughly spoilt grass. As luck would have it, all went well, Mr. Bonzo sighed with relief.

Now it was time for people watching, since we had nothing much else to do, and Mrs. Bonzo had not yet appeared from the department store. There is a large fountain in the middle of a square, a perfect place to sit around, and get pestered by small children, and adults, who take great, delight in pulling them away when they seemed to get too near to me.

The canine fraternity comes in all shapes and sizes; a telecast of the Westminster Dog Show will prove that. I have noticed people also come in all shapes and sizes too. From my vantage point, low down, I saw large, extra large, small, medium and outrageous shapes. Do some of these people know what they look like?

I began to become selective as they approach, I decided anyone over 200lbs should not be allowed to pet me, small children are OK.

Obesity is a problem, so many people have tried dieting, without success, even attempting operating procedures to cut heir weight. Such procedures has elements to it called 'Adjusted Band,' no doubt the side effects could well be ' ' Tle Rolling Gaulstones" and "Bled Zepelin."

I was concerned to see near the fountain a cart with a sign that says Hot Dogs. There is nothing that states what breed they may be' or indeed what size. I suppose the Dachshund would be a natural for this as it is often referred to as the sausage dog.

There is an aroma, wafting across the square, and largely sized people waiting in line, most of them sporting shorts. I have discovered the larger people are, the more they display themselves, and they seem to be constantly eating. How is it my eating habits are limited to morning and evening.?

People get to stand in line, why isn't there a doggy cart, with Hot People for sale, I would like a medium size with relish and mustard please, and a small beer.

Mr. Bonzo decided to get himself a cappuccino, one of his favorite drinks, and stood outside the window of a small café, placing his order, with me in tow.

"Two shots please" I heard, I froze, thinking this is another vet attack.

"Non fat milk, and please make it dry," he continues.

Now I am somewhat bemused at this, how can a wet drink be dry? I thought about getting a latte, but he never asked if I wanted something.

I was beginning to get curious about everything I saw, and as the day passed by, more and more curious.

Mrs. Bonzo finally joined us, it seemed like a week had passed by, as we all took a walk outside the stores around us, peering into shop windows, oohing and aahing over some expensive off the shoulder strapless gown, which I am sure she would never wear. Banging her head against the window with her hand over her eyes, when she gets too close, or the sun disturbs the view, then downing two aspirin because she has a headache.

Humans are incorrigible, somehow it seems like Alice in Window land.

Chapter 6

HOME ALONE

At about thirteen weeks old, I was, as you may be able to tell, getting curious about a lot of things. For example, why is may name Zak, perhaps I would have preferred Oscar or Simon. Why can't puppies choose their own names? When I was waiting at the veterinary surgeons office, I heard humans calling their dogs by names such as Bailey, Fred and once, Eloise, however I don't think in that case, the male Doberman Pincher was impressed.

Today I have been left at home alone. The house is empty Mr. and Mrs. Bonzo have gone off somewhere extolling the virtues Of why they should dart off to one supermarket or the other. Perhaps they will bring me back more treats.

I have decided today not to go ice-skating on the kitchen floor' eat flowers in the garden, or even make another futile attempt at jumping on the bed, in the master bedroom. It has become very embarrassing to me that I cannot reach the bed from any angle, an jump up and down like a frazzled monkey. If I could, this would disturb the occupants of the bed of course, as I would imagine I am on a trampoline, getting some worthwhile exercise.

Since I was on my own it gave me the opportunity to explore at leisure. I rarely visited the bathrooms, but that day I made an exception. I really would like to pull a towel from the rack, and dry myself off, as the two-legged people do, in case I need a shower from the sprinklers. It would be handy to know I can do this. Wheaton Terriers can jump quite early in life and often have a habit of doing so, today I am going to reach the highest I have ever been, snatch a towel and start drying myself, even though I am not as yet wet.

I made several attempts, and eventually, the thing draped itself all over me, so visibility was at zero, and I was constantly tripping over it. I tried a mini version of my whirling dervish, so well executed, that the towel wrapped itself around me twice, I stumbled, and fell head first into a hard object, banging my head. A little dazed I started my jumping routine, for which as you may remember Wheaton's are very adept, and in so doing lifted a lid of some sort.

You must remember I still could not see anything with this double wrapping around me, I felt like an Indian Ghurka whose turban has slipped over his face. If you think about it, this is not something you see very often, at least not in our house.

Here I was blindfolded by a bathroom towel jumping up and down and lifting a lid, which is attached to I don't know what, could be the hamper, or the toilet lid, or something quite foreign to me.

Whilst trying to discover this momentary bane, I hit a lever of some sort, with my head, and tumbled into a pool of water. Suddenly, more water poured on top of me, and I was very wet. I struggled in the darkness to get out of the water, and climb over the edge of the bowl.

Dripping wet, I thought this a very good time to experiment with my towel to see if I can dry myself, in case of need.

Next thing to do, I thought would be attack the hamper, and with great gusto minus the towel, I raced headlong into the side of the wicker basket, whereupon it fell over and out spilled various pieces of dirty laundry, which in my new found wet condition gave me the great opportunity to try to wash and dry.

I did not have much success, but managed to avoid the underwear, which may have proven to be a blessing in disguise. In any event washing it all was easy, drying, was a little more difficult.

This was a good time to move on to the second bedroom, only slightly wet, and explore in there. I am bemused by the noise that is emitted from a large black object that Mr. Bonzo sits at, on occasion. The sounds are not particularly melodic and he seems to make them with his hands, placed in the front. One time he placed me on his lap while sitting on a small stool, and I saw there were black and white objects all in a row. I do remember the noise was a little sweeter than his shofar blowing attempt. I remember he called it a piano. It apparently is a digital piano and sits underneath the bedroom window.

I managed to jump on the stool, and make that as wet as possible, and went in search of piano keys, but they were nowhere to be found. I sat down and pondered the situation, but the reader should be advised, without my bewildered look. I cannot fathom out where those keys went.

In a moment of inspiration, I noticed a lid. It seems pretty heag to lift with my nose, which I thought would be a problem until aided and abetted by my front paws, I could get it to move. With a little extra effort, I manage to get it up around my ears, which with the rest of my face was now buried in darkness under the lid. It is at point my sincerest hope I can hold on before it comes crashing down on me, which I thought would not be a pretty sight.

With keys now before me, I am ready to play. I have had no lessons, don't know one key from another, but it's worth a try. I ponder as to what shall I play, the Wheaton Tell Overture, or since the piano is under the window open for passers by to peer at, how about How Much is that Doggie in the Window.

Unfortunately for me, at the very time I was to make my debut, I heard the garage door open, which is a sign the Bonzos have returned, and I should quickly disappear somewhere, or greet them with an endearing look of how I missed them. I chose neither, since I could not jump off the piano stool.

They entered the house and were surprised to find I was not sitting like good little boy at the kitchen door awaiting their entrance.

"Zak, where are you" I heard, trying to make my concert debut at Carnegie Hall I said to myself. appeared in the bedroom with a look of disbelief.

"Zak, what have you been up to" exclaimed Mrs Bonzo, "You are all wet" she went on, Mr Bonzo was motionless, as I might have expected. Still dripping wet, I tried a wry smile, but in view of the circumstances I should have known better.

"Zak, you cannot ruin the house like this" said Mr Bonzo "Put a lid on it."

Isn't that amazing all morning I had been trying to take a lid off.

Chapter 7

A WALK IN THE NEIGHBORHOOD

Every evening when the Bonzos returned from their daily routine at the office, we started another routine as Mr. Bonzo took me for a walk. As soon as I heard the closet door open and the jingling of the leash I know it was time for "Zak, walkies."

Apparently this daily event could only take place when it is fair weather, which is most of the time, but we never go in the rain. Some time ago I decided to get even for this, by going out into the garden when it rains. As soon as I entered the house, Mr. Bonzo would run for a towel to dry me, as that task is completed, I would immediately run out again in the garden to get all wet again. My record is three times before the sliding door is shut, to prevent further fun on my part.

Each evening we had a tug of war over which direction we were to pursue. I won most of the time, but every now and again I let Bonzo have his way, it is good for him you know. I love to see the smile on his face, when he thinks he is training me, particularly as we cross a street and he booms "Sit" on arriving at the edge of the sidewalk. Occasionally I would sit down just for a rest. It makes him feel good too!

Our neighborhood like most, is a very pleasant place in which to stroll, there are numerous bushes I can get my head stuck in, lots of grass to roll in, and a plethora of fire hydrants. I can remember the first time I encountered a fire hydrant, as if it was yesterday, actually it was yesterday.

While pulling with all my might, and then suddenly coming to a grinding halt, or sniffing something that resembles bird droppings I sighted a yellow object about thirty feet away. I ran with all the speed of a gazelle Mr Bonzo in tow, and suddenly froze as I saw this

30

diminutive yellow object staring me in the face. I jumped back about three feet stepping on my handler's toes and took a good look at this thing.

It resembled a something you would find in a Science Fiction movie, Revenge of the Fire Hydrants or Attack of the Killer Water Spout.

Mr Bonzo started to explain to me what in fact it was, but I still froze.

Gradually I crept nearer to it, moving at a snails pace in case it attacked me. I sniffed, and frankly was not amused to find it had an aroma of dog pee, quite useless to me as I still haven't lifted my leg for those situations.

"Zak, come away, its only a fire hydrant" exclaimed Mr Bonzo, but I was still curious about it.

Occasionally one met up with other dogs, some elderly, some quite sprightly, as they seem perfectly well behaved along side their owners.

I met a cocker spaniel one time, very light in color, and extremely light in the brain I think, he kept on barking at me for no reason at all, I just ignored him. Another time, there was this large animal lurching its way toward me, followed by a gray haired man, Stumbling, frantically holding on to the longest leash I have ever seen, I believe it was a bull mastiff, it was far too heavy for it's owner and he knew it, maybe someday I might emulate him, and drag Mr Bonzo around the neighborhood.

By comparison 1 am really a marshmallow, at least on the outside, with a dose of Mexican jumping beans on the inside, which allows me to spring up and down with great spirit, and annoy people and other dogs. At that time I could leap to a reasonable height and look as though I am going to bite. Since I have grown, and now weigh around twenty three pounds I could knock a human back on the heels, and make them aware I can reach the private parts, at least if I practice. Today I just didn't feel in the mood.

We moved along, returning to my habits of eating fallen leaves finding sticks to chew and the most luxurious of treats getting my face dirty in dried bushes, when I noticed a small black dog in the' distance. It's owner carefully shepherding the animal on the sidewalk with great aplomb. As we neared each other, I sensed a reticence to meet, on the part of the owner, an elderly lady, dressed in a white raincoat and a hat, with pictures of small dogs on it.

We soon came face to face however, and it was Mrs. Raincoat who greeted us first.

What a lovely dog" she pronounced, "What is it?" she asked Suffice to say by now you know, this was getting tiresome, but Bonzo obliged with the usual Soft Coated Wheaten Terrier routine.

"Well" she said, ' 'This is Duncan, he is a West Highland Terrier" Mr. Bonzo nodded his approval of little Duncan.

He is five years old" she continued.

"What's your dogs name?" she said

"Zak" came the obvious reply

"Duncan was a champion you know, on the East Coast" she went on.

"How old is Zak" she continued

"Just over four months" was the reply.

I looked Duncan up and down and decided his legs are too short, I mean really short. Champions should have long legs, and not stand there as if he was being judged at a dog show. I jumped all over him, and smothered his face with my paws. He didn't move an inch. I barked as loudly as I could and still he didn't move a muscle. What kind of champion are you I thought.

Even Mr. Bonzo was surprised at my behavior, although secretly I think he was impressed, I was not afraid.

Mrs. Raincoat explained, "He is trained to stand still, for shows and events.

Well we see about that, I said to myself, as I moved back three steps and lunged at him. Still he didn't move, so I gave him a left hook with my paw, and followed that with a right uppercut. At this point I really thought he was stuffed, based on a lack of movement, I mean he might as well be stuffed. Mrs Raincoat was not amused.

"Duncan, come away" she said disapprovingly.

"Zak, behave yourself" the voice of doom supposedly in my corner bellowed. Champion indeed I thought, if he ever grows longer legs, I'd challenge him to a duel at dawn.

Mr Bonzo bade his farewell, as he tugged on my leash, Mrs. Raincoat stepped away in the opposite direction. I thought Dunce was just like the fire hydrant, it didn't move either."

Chapter 8

RITUALS

There are some things that took place every day, come rain or shine. For example each morning, the Bonzos stood at the bathroom counter, each looking in the mirror, one shaving the other applying make up.

The fun started when one of them entered the shower, with hot water running and a steamy air about the place, it was a wonderful time to grab all the towels, shake them furiously in one's mouth and disappear with them into another room. It is often said the chase is more exciting than anything, and so it became each morning as a nude Mr. Bonzo and a scantily clad Mrs. Bonzo follow me. One time I was banished from the bathroom in the belief I wouldn't do that again, will humans ever learn.

Mrs. Bonzo is a serious make up artist, and by that I mean with facial expressions that would scare a ghost, as she peers into the mirror, from an agonizingly close distance. If I tugged on her robe she would stop and give me a smile, tickle me, or just rub my fur. I came to consider this my morning bathroom activity. Whenever I needed a little comfort she was always there petting me, talking to me as if I could understand, and showing affection, which is why I leapt up and down when her back was turned and nipped at her rear end, it was my way of showing affection.

Mr Bonzo battled with a hair drier each day, which always seems so hot, for the life of me I cannot understand why his head doesn't catch fire. It is probably because he sprays something on it afterward that cools it down. Mrs. Bonzo also doused her hair with a spray, but what I can't understand, is that she doesn't set her head on fire first.

When I first came to the Bonzo household, I was not aware of the ritual that follows the drier, it is the after shave moment. I soon learnt when this is applied, an odor wafts through the air that could probably kill locusts, now I run for cover as soon as the cap comes off the bottle. Occasionally Mrs. Bonzo does the same.

I still haven't come to grips with the fact, that humans put clothes on, and the canine fraternity do not, other than those silly coats sold in pet stores. Watching humans get dressed can be very interesting. Mr. Bonzo always had problems getting his pants on, Mrs. Bonzo likewise adorning herself with a bra, now that's a contraption I would not want to wear.

Some days I longed for the locust killer odor, as the trash was taken out. As much as I like to follow everyone wherever they go' this is one time I can resist the urge. Mr. Bonzo always complains when it is time for this ritual, as he often states "There are six billion people in the world, yet I must be unique, since I am the only one who can take our trash out.

On weekends I was put in the back of the car, to be merely a passenger, as the weekly trip to the cleaners was organized. It was all opportunity for me to exercise my lungs, at the guy who places the cleaning in the back of the car, whenever this occurred I stood on my hind legs peering over the back seat and barked. I was always and still am very protective of the car, but logic prevailing and I don't really know why, it is not my car. Other than that, it was not too exciting an adventure. However on our return to the house, it a was perfect chance to bite at the plastic wrapping, drag freshly cleaned clothes around the floor, and parade around the bedroom with a discarded hanger in my mouth.

I am not keen on plastic wrapping, but Mr. Bonzo is less than enthusiastic, often cursing at the man who invented Saran Wrap. You should see him scissors in hand cutting anything that is shrink wrapped, using profanity as he tries to tear a piece of plastic apart with his bare hands, he looked at me once and said "In the future Zak, children will have to learn to carry scissors with them through life, and learn how, at birth, just to open something that is shrink wrapped in plastic."

The washer and drier is off limits to me, I could hear the strange noises, but have never been privy to the machines that make them, but it was quite a treat watching the Bonzos carry their clean laundry back to the bedroom and drop a few items in my path as I followed them. I sat quite contented as I heard Mr Bonzo vent his rage when a sock or two is missing, or he spotted me with one of his under shorts wrapped round my head, although not something that will ever enhance my image.

Every other day there was that terrible ritual of brushing me, why do I have to be brushed? As soon as the brush comes out of its resting place in the cupboard, I usually ran for my life. I have been known to hide in the garden, even run at sixty miles per hour around and around the living room, knowing the Bonzos will stop chasing before I get tired. I have to admit, though once in a while brushing is not so bad, except when they do my paws, and the back of my legs. I think they scrape the barbeque grill the same way.

The good news is, I get a treat if I stand still and do nothing, while they pride themselves on what a good job they have done on me, the bad news is, this can mean another ritual, having my photograph taken.

The Bonzos recently acquired a new digital camera, which they have been trying to understand how to use, so far with little success. It took at least two weeks I think to get the shrink wrapping off it, and Mr Bonzo cut himself with the scissors a couple of times. One piece got stuck to his rear end, and Mrs. Bonzo in concert with myself decided not to tell him.

The problem with having my photo taken is, most of the time I had to sit down and sit still, not an easy thing for a fun loving five month old puppy, and frankly it was be pretty boring. If some of the shots come out as expected, the Bonzos might well go into ecstasy, even showing me the finished article. Why should I care, I'll see them once, and they will never let me see them again, they will look at them many times. I bet they will never take a photograph of me with a coat hanger in my mouth, or pulling a towel to shreds.

It would be nice once in a while to be adventurous, get away from the norm, do something different. I'll have to see what I can do about that, remember, all work and no play can make Zak a dull boy.

Chapter 9

BEYOND THE GATE

Monday is the day the trash is collected from our house, and I remember the first time I heard the truck advancing down the street, sounding like a herd of thundering elephants, I ran for my life. The trash cans are collected from the side of the house, through a wooden gate. I of course now a little older, usually run into the garden, round to the side of the house to watch the trash man pick up the large cans. For me barking is mandatory, not an option when this occurs.

On this particular Monday, I had a piece of luck. The gate was left open, something the trash collector had not done before. I waited for the elephant herd to depart, and stuck my nose through the gate, I could see no one. was a wonderful opportunity for me to take a stroll on my own. Flhe Bonzos of course were not at home, I was free to explore the world.

I walked to the corner of the street, stopping of course on the grass for sniffing exercises, and turned toward the main thoroughfare. Mr. Bonzo had taken me on the leash many times toward the front guard gate of the complex so I knew my way around, but that day I was as free as a bird.

On our walks I was always fascinated to hear the front gate open, it would creak like a door that needed some oil. As I approached the gate, it opened, the creaking began as a car drove through, so I took my chance and ran through past the guard and into mainstream life. I felt good about myself, and since the weather was pleasant, I thought a stroll in the park would do me good, so I headed in that direction, well I thought it was the park, but somehow, I must have missed the street, with all the noise of the traffic passing me. I probably lost my sense of direction. I was in fact at a crossroads, where it seemed some cars were moving and some standing still. I am not sure why some were stationary, but maybe the colored lights had something to do with it. I recognized a couple of stores in the distance, where patiently I had waited outside in the car for "The Bonzos to return.

I crossed the road, without looking left or right, and heard the screeching of brakes and glass shattering, as a couple of cars danced together, but I paid no attention to them. After all this was going to be my day out on my own. As I reached the other side and continued on my merry way, the sound of ambulances could be head Everyone on the street seemed to stop and watch them pass by, I didn't bother.

I came to another set of colored lights, and went speeding across as fast as my legs could carry me. Once again I heard the screeching of brakes, and wondered does this always happen when you cross the road?

In the corner of my eye I spotted a familiar sight, a regular haunt of the Bonzos, Starbucks Coffee. Hmm I thought I have never managed to enter this establishment, it is high time I saw what all the fuss is about. It was about this time I heard another ambulance speeding by, with sirens blaring. Well I said to myself it is a busy day for paramedics.

The door of the coffee house was closed, and as hard as I pressed my nose up against the glass, I couldn't open it. I would have to wait for a two legged human, to go in or out. It didn't take long, as a young lady with a tray and several paper cups emerged, unfortunately her timing and mine were not exactly together, as she pushed to open the door, I raced through, and she seemed to trip over me landing face down. All the cups dispersed in different directions, how clumsy of her I thought, however she can come in again and get some more.

The aroma inside was distinctly unpleasant to me, however as I looked around me between the maze of legs, and people running to the aid of the unfortunate young lady between the front door and the side walk, I somehow backed in to a display of mugs and cups that toppled over. It was about this time that I heard the cry

"Someone call 911" and before you could say ambulance, those blasted sirens could be heard again, and a red truck arrived with paramedics. Now I know that in the USA there are days for everything, Mothers Day, Fathers Day, Presidents Day, Labor Day, Memorial day, and so on, so I surmised this must be Paramedics Day. Pretty soon there will be some kind of day of note, three hundred and sixty five days a year, with a day off on leap years.

With so much confusion around me, I thought this is not the way to spend my day off, so I departed. I trotted around to the front and decided to miss out on the activities, particularly with all those flashing lights, and hysteria, and move on toward a large building where people were pushing carts in and out of doors that opened on their own. This was looking better for me I didn't have to wait for someone to open the door, as I stepped up to the front, it automatically opened.

Much better I thought, if all doors were like this four legged animals could go in and out at will. I made a note to remember that this place is called a market.,

I entered a world of lots of people standing in line, express lanes, mostly closed, push carts, and a lot of seemingly fat people, mostly wearing shorts. There were several smells intriguing to a young puppy, so further investigation was a must. I turned right, which apparently most people do when entering a market and made my way toward the bakery. It was at this point I heard someone say "Look there's a dog in here" I barked at this "I am a Soft Coated Wheaton Terrier, not a dog."

This brought more people to the scene, including a couple in white coats, screaming "Catch him." I couldn't believe Paramedics Day can be so cruel to Wheatons.

It was a time to run, so I made for an aisle, which to my amazement had shelves of doggy treats. I stopped momentarily, snatched one and continued down the aisle. As I reached the end, I made a swift turn to the left, making sure the treats were firmly held in my mouth, and ran down the next aisle. Unfortunately an elderly couple, one with a walking cane were just about to turn around when I arrived, and the old gentleman fell as I took his feet from under him. The elderly lady with him fainted.

39

ZAK

Pandemonium ensued, as I merrily trotted toward the front door' from whence I entered, as people shouted, call 911, and some even suggested get the dog !

Back in the parking lot, I decided I really should look for the park, as yet another ambulance arrived, and perhaps rid myself of all this noise and commotion, and bask in the tranquility between the trees. Just as humans dream of beaches and white sands on desert islands, it was becoming a passion for me to find the park, and I could snuggle between the blades of grass and chew on my doggie treats.

As I arrived at the crossroads I first encountered, an ambulance was departing, and life seemed to be returning to normal on this busy street. Some cars were standing still, some moving, people were waiting to cross the road, some waiting at those colored lights so long, they packed a lunch, as for me time and tide waits for no man or Wheaton, so I crossed. Luckily there was no brake screeching, or for that matter paramedics needed, so I ran in search of my little heaven.

Running up the hill, that I had previously ran down, what seemed so long ago, I spotted a large group of trees, so I headed in that direction. As I turned a corner I was amazed to find a policeman on a motor cycle, holding some kind of machine pointing it at cars passing by. Instinctively I knew this must be some kind of gun that makes vehicles crash into one another, causing screeching, shattered glass and the arrival of paramedics.

This was a wrong that I had to put right. I have seen on television people picket for what they think is right, or throw bricks in windows, admittedly I had never seen Wheatons, Labradors, or West Highland Terriers do this, but I thought I would try and prevent this officer causing more havoc. I bet little Duncan would not attempt to be a knight in shining armor, I guess he's more the silent type. Somehow, I just simply had to stand up for my breed.

The officer seeing me, smiled and continued pointing his machine, I leapt with all my strength upon him, using much of my Mexican jumping bean assets, to knock him off his motor cycle, and just as quickly as I leapt, I ran away toward home, thinking, through all this mayhem I somehow lost my treats that were in my

40

mouth from my outing to the market. I looked behind me to see the officer waving frantically, and shouting at me, and some smoke apparently coming from his motor cycle which appeared on it's side. No wonder there was all that commotion because of him, he couldn't even control his own motor cycle.

As I approached the gates that earlier I had crossed alone for the first time, I couldn't help thinking it was nice to return home, so much noise, and confusion goes on beyond the gates, it's enough to make a Wheaten homebound.

Later that day the Bonzos returned home muttering something about the carnage in the streets according to news reports, attributed to person or persons unknown. They seemed concerned at the events for that day, for my part I just ignored them.

Chapter 10

DREAMS

Sometimes when the Bonzos are in bed sleeping, and snoring, they seem to be in another world. I have often wondered when I see them like this, what are they dreaming about? You can tell they are dreaming, a little twitch here and there, a momentary noise or two.

I can't imagine why, but I bet they often look at me as I lay prostrate on the floor, with my belly toward the ceiling, saying to one another I wonder what he's dreaming about. Have you ever looked at an animal sleeping, with that thought? I bet the Bonzos wonder what I get up to all day when they are gone, and don't give a thought to me wondering where it is they go to everyday.

I can give the reader some insight at least, although dreams are hard to remember, some stay with me, and repeat themselves, like the one I keep having where I am master and the Bonzos are my pets. Silly as that may seem, it is a dream I like. I think it would be wonderful for me to talk to them and they make interesting faces when they can't understand what I am saying or should I say barking about.

In my dream the Bonzos have two dishes, both silver, one for water, bottled of course, and one with their food. mne latter I fill for them every day, with crunchy small objects that look like croutons and something that comes from a can, chicken and rice or on good days beef. They stoop to lap up the delights of dinner, while I watch lovingly, they like me, are very protective of their dishes, no one may come close while eating.

When I am eating, it is always cookies and doggie treats, now there is a dream worth remembering.

One of the drawbacks, is after a while they go into the garden and do what has to be done, and I have to clean up after them, I call this "Poop Patrol."

Somehow the dream always ends with reality, as I am stirred by deep voices in my head clearly telling me "Wake up Zak, its all a dream."

I once had a dream of going to the vet, and giving him an injection, but that was all too short, so was the one about me giving the handlers there, a bath. That raises another dream of mine, not to give in to people who want to blow dry me, by letting them put me in the unenviable position of being strung up to a post, I thought hanging had been abolished, while on a table from which I can't jump, due to it's height, while they fuss all over me with a hot blow dryer, and a brush.

I have visited the vet on more than one occasion, once or twice just to make sure I am healthy, this usually is a short visit. One time we saw a vet I had not seen before, Dr. Fox, and this got me thinking, all vets names should have animal connections such as Dr' Lamb, or Dr. Rabbit, this particular visit was just a minute or two, so I thought he should have been called Dr. Dolittle !

Have you ever noticed, how good dreams seem to end quickly. Not so long ago I was in the middle of a wonderful spell, dreaming about a ménage a trios, when I awoke to find myself on the bed with the Bonzos, and they telling me to get off it!

On the bed during the day sits a stuffed dog they call Madeleine. I think it's a terrier of some sort, and there for decorative purposes, every now and then Mrs. Bonzo lets me snuggle up to it, as if care. The thing is stuffed, it won't move, and to add insult to injury I was recently neutered, now there's a bad dream, so snuggling up to this immovable object is no fun for me. It doesn't do anything, despite the gesticulations of Mrs. Bonzo petting it, as if real, and I am supposed to like this little game.

Recently I dreamt about walking around the neighborhood, not attached to a leash of course, and sniffing around the trees and lamp poles, trying to catch the smells of other dogs. Dogs love to catch the aroma from a previous participant in the pee and poop game. Now if this is true, who was the first dog ? I dreamt it was

43

me, and I was hoisted on the shoulders of dogs everywhere holding a large silver cup, as the champion dog that started it all.

One of my favorite dreams, I called Lord Wheaton and the Brittania Grill, as I imagined myself getting dressed for dinner on the QE2, sailing from New York to Southampton, about to taste the delights of scintillating cocktails, and a delicious meal. Decked out in a tuxedo, bow tie and all, my entrance to the Grill spectacular as the heads turned upon my entrance. I think I had this dream because I heard the Bonzos once talking about the time they sailed on the revered ship, but spent the majority of their time getting lost aboard, trying to find their cabin.

On a more mundane level, I have also dreamt about taking a language course in Spanish, so when I bark at the gardeners that come to the house every week they will know I been business!

I would like to have a dream about vacuum cleaners, every time the cleaner comes to the house and takes this machine out of the closet, it scares the living daylights out of me. The noise is not something I like, and at seven months old, if truth be known, I was still afraid of this thing. I ran as far as my legs would carry me, and still do. I wished I knew how to end this misery.

A big change in my life came when I was taken to a new place for a bath and cut. Up to now my hair has been growing longer and I felt and looked shaggy. A real Wheaten cut was ordered for me, and I came out looking very different with shorter hair, and much lighter in color, I had lost the dark hairs, and now appearing very much like the Wheaten dogs you see at shows.

The first time I looked in the mirror when we arrived home, I did not recognize myself. That night I dreamt I was paraded around the ring, and caught the eye of the judges at Madison Square Garden, at the Westminster Dog Show, and was announced as Supreme Champion, it was a lovely dream and all too short, so was my haircut.

Dreams, it's the stuff of which life is not made.

Chapter 11

CAUSING HAVOC

Some days I just felt like causing a little havoc, there again some days it just seemed to fall into my lap. At eight months I was stretching my ability to not only to be more curious, but also to take advantage of situations as they arise.

Take the time Mr. Bonzo put me in his new car, which is black in color, shiny and squeaky clean as new cars tend to be, and perfectly primed for muddy paws and occasional car sickness.

As usual I was relegated to the back seat, with a new towel neatly laid out, for me to sit on. "Zak, do not jump about like a lunatic" he proclaimed, "Stay on the towel, and sit like a good boy, I don't want you messing up the car.

This was a clear signal in my book, to pace up and down like a caged lion, and run from one side of the back seat to the other. mun calmly sit looking out of the window, as if nothing had happened.

We were on our way to a pet store to pick up some doggie food, a trip I enjoy very much. The smells in that place are a sheer delight for a Wheaten, and I assume for all breeds. There is one aisle after another full of treats, toys and various kinds of bags containing all the ingredients necessary for a puppy to grow, obtain a fine bone structure, clear bad breath, and generally if allowed to... pig out.

This visit was toward the end of the day, and my senses kicked in as we approached the parking lot, and I realized how close we were to the store. Mentally I was gearing up for a mad rush through aisle two, where the treats and toys reside, so by the time we parked I was preparing myself as if a sprinter at the Olympics ready to come out of the blocks.

As the back door opened, I gave Mr. Bonzo little chance of grabbing at my leash, by vaulting a foot or two in the air, using the towel as traction, and with great speed landed out onto the pavement. The towel landed on Mr. Bonzo, who was taken aback by all this, because I had never been able to jump out of the car before. His last car was a tall contraption, so it was always difficult for me to get in and out without assistance, this one although similar was not as formidable a hurdle.

Without breaking a step, I burst through the open doors, straight to aisle two, some distance behind me I could hear a muffled cry from Mr. Bonzo "Zak, stop, stop running." It was a muted cry, since I suppose it must be hard to bellow properly with a towel halfway over your face.

In any event I was not about to stop with such prizes ahead Of me, bones, plastic balls, furry animals and so on, but I stopped to grab a treat, from a low shelf on the aisle. Regrettably Mr. Bonzo caught up with me, and once again he held my leash at a time when I least wanted him to, a common occurrence in my life.

Now that I am nearly at my full weight, it is not too hard to pull Mr. Bonzo around by sheer speed alone, as he hung on to the leash, and with so many smells to investigate, I ran in different directions at breakneck speed, with Mr. Bonzo in tow.

Onlookers would smile at my trailing, and sometimes panicking Englishman, people stared as we sped by and generally fell about into a heap laughing when I went round a corner, and he continued on a direct path into a sign reading Large Cages On Sale. The good news is all the doors were closed, the bad news is, a small precocious three year old girl was peering into one of them as the assailant landed on top of her. The little girl started crying loudly, a better description would be bawling.

The little girl's mother grabbed her, as Mr. Bonzo apologized profusely, and all was forgotten and forgiven as they petted me. "What kind of dog is that?" asked Mother of the Precocious one.

"A sift kilted whoten tirrier" replied Mr. Bonzo.

Not exactly as he intended but with a combination of recent dental work, and a brush with a large wire cage, the response wasn't exactly understandable.

People tend to believe what you tell them, so it was no surprise to find Mother and the little precocious one, whose name turned out to be Cherise, accepted the reply.

"How old is he? asked Cherise.

"Oight months" was how Mr. Bonzo responded, with his mouth twisted and in some pain.

What's his name" asked another little boy standing nearby.

Attempting some humor Mr. Bonzo tried with a wry smile, "We don't know, he can't talk yet" but due to the entanglement with wire cages and possibly as a result, of the new shape of his mouth, the little boy thought he heard "Guido Donut Con Tokyo" and he may well have done, whereupon he suggested I didn't look Japanese.

For the uninitiated pedigree papers have names that sound very precocious and not the names people call their dogs, so the question of my call name did not come as a surprise. I have pedigree papers and my parents, grandparents and forefathers have exotic sounding names that I can't pronounce, for that matter neither can Mr. and Mrs. Bonzo.

The small fair haired youngster unfortunately despite his handsome appearance had the misfortune to stutter, and his speech was impaired with a lisp, so his utterances came as somewhat indistinct to the ensemble that now gathered.

What we all heard was "Iz iz that his real name or or his cell name?" thinking perhaps I might be an escaped dog convict.

"Hos cull name is Zik" said Mr. Bonzo.

"Zi.. .Zi.K" stuttered, little fair hair.

"Yes, Zik thit's hos cull name" was just the kind of reply that the ensemble was waiting for with which to greet me. "Zik" could be heard from several different people all trying to get my attention, including Mother Precocious, who chipped in with ' 'What a strange name".

"No," responded Mr. Bonzo, his numb is Zik."

"Wh, wh, where does he come from" inquired the small boy who was beginning to irritate Mr. Bonzo, and for that matter I wasn't too happy staying in one spot for so long.

"Eye Oh Wah" was the response.

As this scintillating conversation was proceeding, Mr. Bonz0 grabbed a couple of bags of doggie food, one under each arm, while holding my leash. Good time to run again I decided, and all this standing around was making me antsy.

With two eight-pound bags, it cannot be easy to maneuver at the end of a leash, and that proved to be the case as I made a left turn, on two legs, at a speed I had not reached before, the bags split, and out tumbled what was to be the next two weeks of breakfast and dinner.

Crunching noises could be heard throughout the store, it was as though heavy snow had fallen, and humanity was making it's way across a frozen tundra.

Despite the giggles from the precocious Cherise and Fair Hair, the more adult of the group were not amused, particularly one newcomer to the group, intent on finding out why the crowd had gathered, he slid legs first into a large outside dog kennel, and despite the fact there was a significant price reduction on this day, it was not something he wanted to investigate or purchase.

As the call went out over the loudspeaker system "Mess to clean up on aisle two, three .oh and aisle four and five" the management and staff appeared on the scene to mop up, and calm things down, and hopefully restore order. Usually at times like these, I like to move in a different direction, there is no point in waiting around for some- thing to happen, you have to make it happen.

Mr. Bonzo was most apologetic, although he must have been in some discomfort with some his teeth protruding from his upper lip. He grabbed two more bags, and we made our way to the cash register.

There waiting impatiently was a line of six or seven people, it seems the machine that runs credit cards, was not in service. Standing behind the counter was the usual checker, a teenager, with obviously years of experience at handling crisis situations, such as credit card machines that don't work, and putting small round rolls of toilet paper in the register, for receipts, when they run out of paper.

Eventually, we stood at the head of the line, me frantic to go on a rampage again, Mr. Bonzo holding bags of food, my leash wrapped around his body, so he couldn't move, and a flustered teenager, who had just recovered from a string of abuse due to circumstances beyond her comprehension.

As we arrived, she was inserting one of those small toilet rolls in the cash register and taking her time doing it.

"We're not holding you up, while we are waiting patiently" inquired Mr. Bonzo.

" The machine is not working" she proclaimed.

"Neither is my mouth" was the response from the heavy laden Mr. Bonzo, somewhat dismayed, you see he has a golden rule, not to appear in front of counters when the staff are under the age of thirty.

Life has taught him teenagers at the cash register, or assistinc in sales, are usually not of the ilk he responds to very well, based on as he might put it service you used to get years ago."

The irony of it all is that the Bonzos in their property tax bill pay some special tax to assist the education of children at the local schools, only to see them grow up leave school, and stand before them at shop counters, so thatMr. Bonzo can refuse to have anything to do with them.

"Cash or check only" stated the well under thirty not much over sixteen year old.

"I don't have my chick book with me" came the reply, a little clearer than before, he seemed to be recovering.

"I don't care about your little black book, cash or check only" she said with some venom.

We paid the young lady, and as we were about to depart, she said "Do you need any help with those bags."

"No" I thought, "We can cause enough havoc on our own, thank you.

Ah well, on some occasions life can be just a bawl of Cherise.

Chapter 12

WORDS AND PHRASES

The Bonzos were then and still are constantly talking to me, Mrs. Bonzo in particular, as if I understand everything she says. Wheatens like other dogs tend to latch on to certain phrases, that are repeated and stay in one's memory.

I have come to recognize such phrases, such as "Get off the Sofa" or "Zak don't do that." Of course such basic and menial orders like, "Sit" and "Stay" are commonly remembered by all canines, and I tend to oblige just for some peace and quiet. However some phrases I just can't understand.

Take the case of what must be a Viking Warrior from a Nordic Saga, or an ex King of Norway... Hoodahel. So often I hear Mr• Bonzo say this to his loving spouse, and it gets me quite perplexed, My understanding is that this Hoodahel is extremely well versed in all matters, and is all knowing on any subject.

I can't tell you how many times I have heard him say to Mrs. Bonzo "Hoodahel knows!"

The English language can be very complex to a young puppy, although I am grateful not to have landed in a home that speaks only Chinese or Japanese. Although I have tried to understand it, English that is, so many times I am left wondering. What for example is the difference when, twice a day what goes in my food bowl seems similar, with a few variations, yet one is called breakfast and one, dinner, and the water bowl contains exactly the same water on both occasions.

Why, when we go out, do I hear "Walkies" and yet when they want to take me out later, so I don't get too excited at that moment, when they don't want me to, they call it a stroll, believing I won't understand the difference. I assure you I don't understand the difference.

I have compiled for the reader a list of words and phrases, so you have an understanding of how they are interpreted by a Wheaton Terrier, should you have the good grace, and may I add good fortune to have one as an addition to the family.

Cookie:
A rare treat, that follows an expectation to perform party tricks gratefully and graciously.

Lie Down:
I am tired of playing with you, leave me alone, I am watching TV with a remote in my hand, called a remote because we haven't the remotest idea of how to use it correctly.

Finish the food in your bowl:
There are people starving in Africa, none of whom we know, nor I can't tell you how many times I have heard him say to Mrs. Bonzo "Hoodahel knows!"

The English language can be very complex to a young puppy, although I am grateful not to have landed in a home that speaks only Chinese or Japanese. Although I have tried to understand it, English that is, so many times I am left wondering. What for example is the difference when, twice a day what goes in my food bowl seems similar, with a few variations, yet one is called breakfast and one, dinner, and the water bowl contains exactly the same water on both occasions. Why, when we go out, do I hear "Walkies" and yet when they want to take me out later, so I don't get too excited at that moment, when they don't want me to, they call it a stroll, believing I won't understand the difference. I assure you I don't understand the difference.

I have compiled for the reader a list of words and phrases, so you have an understanding of how they are interpreted by a Wheaton Terrier, should you have the good grace, and may I add good fortune to have one as an addition to the family.

Cookie:
A rare treat, that follows an expectation to perform party tricks gratefully and graciously.

Lie Down:
I am tired of playing with you, leave me alone, I am watching TV with a remote in my hand, called a remote because we haven't the remotest idea of how to use it correctly.

Finish the food in your bowl:
There are people starving in Africa, none of whom we know, nor would we want to, or to whom, if you don't eat it, would we have the irreverence to ship dog food.

If you don't behave, we'll board you at the vet:
We are going on vacation tomorrow, for a few days, you're going to the vet anyway.

Stop Eating the Bushes:
We have to be careful what we eat, so you must.

No Jutnping on the bed:
It would be OK once or twice, but if you did this regularly it would become an annoyance.

Stop Barking.
We can express ourselves, by burping, sneezing, wheezing, coughing, and producing flatulence... you can't.

No Dogs Allowed:
Entrance to all things sublime.

Now when words and phrases are used in sentences usually spoken by humans at a pace faster than a Wheaton can understand, certainly by New Yorkers or those from France who insist on rudeness to visitors, it is strangely ineffective on a canine, and for a Wheaten' impossible to comprehend.

For example, take the French waiter at a nearby Café one day' having just encountered Mr Bonzo and me, at the entrance, with his pseudo French accent:

"Good Moaning" he said

"Good Moaning, do you mean morning" retorted Mr. Bonzo

"Off course" came the reply swiftly

I mentally pictured a golf ball flying into a sand trap, but missed this quickly.

"Table for one and a half" said Mr. Bonzo as he looked at me, then the waiter.

"Monsieur, you cannot bring dog into ze Café."

"Why not?" asks Mr. Bonzo.

"Becoz, we ave food in ere" stated the French exile.

"Of course you have food in here you're a café, no doubt you have ersatz coffee, left over from World War Two, a selection of pastries, and frogs legs, but I assure you Zak isn't going to eat any of it."

"Who is zis Zak person" said the waiter impatiently.

"Ilis Zak person you French imbecile, is my lovely Wheaten Terrier" said a now slightly exasperated Mr. Bonzo.

"Where is it?" inquired the waiter.

"Where's what? Retorted my knight in shining armor.

"Your Wheaten Person Terrier, sacre bleu, are you an idiot?"

"Don't call me an idiot, you puffed up greasy Frenchman" shouted a not so docile Englishman.

"No dogs allowed" I shall say no more...and with that Anglo French relations went on hold, as the waiter strutted toward the back of the Café.

"Come back" Mr. Bonzo was getting red in the face "Why are dogs not allowed, do you have a sign?

"Oui, zer it is" retorted the Frenchman pointing to a small white board in the shape of a French Poodle, located on an easel with three legs. Written in a scrawled handwriting, that probably only those of Gaelic descent could clearly decipher, were the words THE BISTRO....No Dogs Allowed.

You want a sign I will give you a sign, with my middle finger." shouted the waiter.

ZAK

A few moments later another Frenchman appeared from nowhere, and approached us, dressed in a striped T Shirt, black pants and a beret, sporting a pencil thin moustache His name was on his shirt, and apparently it is Bob.

He looked remarkably like the waiter, almost as if he had sprung I into a quick change artist, and donned a French disguise.

"Monsieur, I am the manger of this Café, can I help you?"

"Manger, do you mean manager."

"That is what I said, manger."

At this point you may wonder what I was doing, well for one thing I was sitting quietly with my head shifting east to west, west to east, like they do at Wimbledon, when watching tennis, listening to this commotion, wondering most of the time what the argument was about.

"Why can't I bring my dog into your café? "inquired Mr. Bonzo.

"It is not at all lowed" replied the greasy Frenchman.

"Not at all lowed, do you mean not allowed?"

"Off course."

And so it went on, Mr Bonzo concerned for my well being beat a hasty retreat in frustration.

As we left, Mr. Bonzo continued muttering to himself "They let dogs in cafes in Paris, they even eat them in Asia, why not in our town?

My point here is I didn't want to enter the café, I was led, like a horse taken to water, but I have to admit "No Dogs Allowed" is a sign I will look for in the future, if only to battle for Doggie Rights and avoid greasy Frenchmen.

As for that daily 'Finish the food in your bowl' the Bonzos Often declare to me, I am getting a little uptight on this one. Humans can eat what they want, , when they want, where they want... for me its in the kitchen, out of my bowl, and once in a while they surely must know how I yearn for dinner out, served by an Italian waitress, or a Greek waiter intent on performing Zorba's dance, or at the very least a waitress at Hooters.

I never eat out, can you imagine that, I never get taken out to breakfast, brunch at the Ritz, or for a burger at McDonalds. Sometimes I hear Mrs. Bonzo complain of the same discontent.

All in all, I was still at a loss over the English language and have not as yet succeeded in understanding many words and phrases, and in part because Mr Bonzo changed the sign at the French café, furtively before we left, as the French Resistance disappeared, from THE BISTRO 'No Dogs Allowed' to Bistro NO! ... Dogs Allowed.

Chapter 13

WRITERS BLOCK

Chapter 14

MEMORIES AND BONZOISMS

There was a time when all I had to do was eat, sleep and perform my ablutions in the garden and life was satisfying. As I was getting older, simple things no longer seem to satisfy me, however on the other hand the Bonzos seem to be going in the other direction. Some of my life then and now has been, and seems always will be having to listen to the Bonzos as they reminisce.

I heard them often complain of what they use to do, that now seems an encumbrance to them, and as they are getting older how life has changed. I feel the same way.

Both of them wish they were younger and as Mrs Bonzo often said "We should all be born at eighty, and work our way toward youth, then we would have something to look forward to."

We Wheatens have a relatively short life, so while not complaining, I would rather nurture the best of the few years I have by comparison to humans, toward having a good time, working my way toward adulthood. At least graduate from puppy food, to the larger cans, showing doggie cousins of mine with shiny coats and leaping to great heights as they appear to be superbly fit, from eating whatever is inside the can. The cans purchased for me at the market are small and never contain anything close the announcements made by Mr. Bonzo on retrieving one for my dinner.

"Tonight Zak it's Beouf Stroganoff' he sometimes pronounced with the air of a great European Chef or Steak Tartare, but it always turned out to be a standard Gourmet Dinner or whatever has been plucked from the shelves of the market. Where have those days gone when, he was so pleased to tell me so simply "Dinner's ready."

I am not old enough to reminisce, or sometimes can even remember what happened yesterday, I may as well have Dogsheimers disease, but the Bonzos often put themselves in a state of delirium when they banter on life in their past. It's amazing what humans can remember, and usually most trivial, yet they talk about unobtrusive events in their life, as if they should somehow be frozen in time, and on display at the great museums of the world, along with the Declaration of Independence or the Magna Carta.

Many times such memories evoke belly laughs, giggling and no doubt realms of fantasy, embellished to the point of beyond belief. I just stare at them nonchalantly, and many times walk off in disgust, lay down near the fireplace and dream of Iowa. Humans can be so aggravating.

So many times Mrs. Bonzo breaks a silence with something that only she can find funny because she knows the real meaning of her statement. Usually this is delivered without warning and when ther man nor beast could have expected a crack in the air. Man in this case being Mr. Bonzo, who after years of these kinds of earth shattering moments, has become accustomed.

I had heard them talk before of the time years ago when they were lying in bed, discussing what dog they might like to own. It seems among the candidates was a standard poodle.

"What color?" inquired Mr. Bonzo.

"Black." came the reply.

"What would you call it?" Mr. Bonzo asked.

"Brown?" suggested Mrs. Bonzo.

"Brown, but it would be black." retorted Mr. Bonzo

"Browne with an e." she added.

So it was one evening during a balmy summer, when the air conditioning was going full blast, and Mrs. Bonzo kept complaining of how hot she was, and Mr. Bonzo slouching in his large leather armchair reminding her of how chilly he felt, although dressed for Antarctica, on account of the air conditioner, and two giant ceiling fans spinning as though any moment they would take flight, giving new momentum to the age of the turbo prop airplane.

"I was just thinking of all the places I have lived where I didn't have to leave to go somewhere else" said Mrs. Bonzo.

Mr. Bonzo was transfixed with a blank stare as if rooted in one spot, and a hand grenade was approaching to troops in the trenches, and he should shout "Incoming" There was no reply, and another silence ensued.

Do you remember Mexico" said Mrs. Bonzo starkly and completely out of the blue.

"I think it's south of here" responded Mr. Bonzo.

No, silly I mean do you remember the time we went to Puerto Vallarta?"

"7.30" was the reply, droll to say the least.

"In the morning." he continued.

"Be serious" Mrs. Bonzo continued.

"Hum" said Mr. Bonzo

"I was thinking of that dark night on vacation in Puerto Vallarta, when we drove in that open Jeep we rented, to the restaurant on the beach, and encountered that very large pig in the middle of the road" she said.

"What on earth could have reminded you of that" whispered Mr. Bonzo carefully tucking in his oversized sweatshirt, beneath some large sweat pants, as he reminisced mentally of the days he had a smaller waistline.

"Nothing really" proclaimed Mrs Bonzo, "I was thinking of how things used to be, when we younger" she said in a soft voice. "The places we went to, the fun we had."

As I lay motionless on the living room carpet, I couldn't help noticing all the blotchy circles, where in times gone by I had thrown up. I didn't realize how many shapes I had managed, some large, some small, and many I am sure, the result of which Picasso would have been proud. Half of them I don't remember, a couple I thought I should be content with, for, as a young pup, eating leaves and throwing up was all in a days work. Despite the attentions of a carpet cleaner that arrives once in a while my trademark patterns reappear, although not patented.

"We went to a lot of places" remarked Mr. Bonzo carrying on as if he had no idea I was listening or able to think for myself, "That bloody Jeep was a disgrace" he said. "From what I remember, the gears got stuck we broke down more than once, and had to take a taxi from that restaurant, to get back to the hotel" "Yes and you came completely unglued as I recall" she replied mockingly.

The conversation drifted from one vacation memory to another, with mostly Mrs. Bonzo giggling like a schoolgirl, and Mr. Bonzo displaying one frown of dismay followed by another.

It occurred to me how come they have all these memories, and all I can do is get through one day after another not trying to remember anything since each day seem very much like the last. What happened to the days when as a young puppy I was the center of attention, every move was followed by the eager anticipation of what I might do next, something I rarely knew myself. I used to be a spur of the moment guy, not even I knew, what could take my fancy. Now it's becoming routine, and humdrum, not to mention I don't have someone to talk to, reminisce on moments shared.

It was as if an elderly portly Seventeenth Century Beefeater was making a proclamation in front of the Royal Court, that Mrs Bonzo blurted out "Remember when we were stuck in Paris, the day the Metro was on strike and we couldn't get a cab" she stated amusingly, "We had to walk for miles in the rain to get back to the hotel, pointing in the direction of the Eiffel Tower, for guidance" she continued. What's more I got blisters, and you forgot the umbrella, which I clearly suggested we take with us."

"It's not going to rain you said, perfectly clear day, you can see the Eiffel Tower from our room," you said, well that's because it was only a hundred yards away, and could easily be seen from our window!" the barrage went on and on.

"Could have done with that bloody Jeep from Mexico" responded Mr. Bonzo "With or without gears" he continued, "And we didn't have an umbrella with us on that trip" he concluded.

As I listened patiently, and the chill of the night air approached with the fans still revolving, and creating a tornado that could grace Kansas in the summer, Mr. Bonzo slumping further into his chair, Mrs. Bonzo still delivering her Royal Proclamations, it occurred to me, will I ever have such memories. have someone to talk to, other than the Bonzos, will I be able to conjure up Bonzoisms.

Chapter 15

THEY LOVE ME...BUT NEVER ASK ME

Sometimes time can go past quickly, I have now lived with the Bonzos for some eighteen months, and it is quite clear to me they really love me. How can I tell, they play with me, they pet me, and they constantly dote on me. I am also a true Wheaten color and unrecognizable from early puppy days, but it makes no difference to the Bonzos, they still love me.

Each night there seems to be a public service announcement, as one of them proposes "Time for bed." This is usually followed by a snappy response from the other "Do you want to watch the news in bed." Now I have seen this little ritual night after night, and actually jumped on the bed, many times pulling back the sheets with my now fully grown teeth, and yet not once have I witnessed any newscasters under the covers. In my lifetime with the Bonzos I haven't regarded anything newsworthy from beneath the sheets.

Although on one occasion I do recall both of them in what they call intimacy. While locked in love, I sat by the side of the bed, with my legs slightly apart, gaping jaws releasing the largest of yawns. Mr. Bonzo turned to me and said "Am I boring you" and with that Mrs. Bonzo remarked "No, its OK."

Who else but the Bonzos would let me watch them get undressed at night before they go to bed, not a pretty sight, but sometimes interesting. Only Mrs. Bonzo would let me sit on her lap as if a precious child, and cuddle up to her for hours on end, soothing my brow, and whispering sweet nothings in my ear.

On one inelegant evening, just as they were about to retire for the night, and undressing in the bedroom. Mr. Bonzo looked at me and opened the conversation with "Zak, only dogs look at humans the way you're looking at me right now, cats just seem disinterested, why is that?"

It is as if I understood the meaning of life, as I stared at him, or something close to that because he continued with "Why are you looking at me like that?"

I suspect he was expecting some sort of reaction, but all I did was lower my head and stare more intently at him. Dogs are prone to doing that. "There you go again Zak" he said, "Why, why are you looking at me like that?"

I'm not sure he realized at this time his shirt was floating ungraciously toward the floor, or one sock was off, and the other still partly adhered to an upturned left foot, while hopping on one leg and vehemently lurching toward the dresser. Under these circumstances anyone would lower their head, and once the undershorts came off even Mrs. Bonzo rolled her eyes In disbelief, and yet she had time to pet me, It is moments like these that I know they love me.

I sleep in the bedroom, close to the sliding door, near, Mrs' Bonzo. It is comforting to know that Mr. Bonzo is close at hand, as he snores and blows hot air through the night.

Depending on the weather, the door is open or closed, or partly open or partly closed. It's like a glass of water that's either half full or half empty, or maybe the glass is too big. How is it they never ask me if I want it open.

Sometimes Mr. Bonzo at some unearthly hour of the night closes the sliding door in his pajamas, which is a strange place to have a door...in his pajamas. This infuriates Mrs. Bonzo who adores open doors, cold winds, air conditioning at full blast, speedy fans, rainstorms, thunder, lightening and jewelry.

Based on the cooling trend that the household has now endured for some time, Mr. Bonzo is convinced they will never have sex in the tropics, Mrs. Bonzo is convinced they may never have sex again at home or anywhere else. I have noticed Mr. Bonzo searching the internet for vacation packages in Alaska.

On a day that turned out to be Mr. Bonzo's birthday, he commented how disgusted he was that his age and the outside temperature seemed to be compatible.

Mrs Bonzo suggested it must be very hot out, to which he replied "Not in Anchorage."

Whenever I am put in the car they never ask me to plan a trip. We always go where they want to go. I get fed when they want to feed me, sometimes I feel like saying, not now, how about in an hour.

Once in a while it would be nice if I could suggest a beach party, Or a night out on the town, but I have no say in the matter. I wonder what would happen if I could convey that I really could go for a facial, massage and a sun tanning salon, would it be too much to ask?

Whenever they watch TV, it's always a program they like, well I would like to watch the Animal Planet Channel please, followed by Dog Day Afternoon, and an all day special on Lassie and Rin Tin Tin, who of course became idols to the Doggie World.

Wouldn't it be nice if I could organize a party for many of my neighborhood friends, whom I still meet occasionally around our local streets, and invite them over one evening for beer and pretzels. Chances are they would all show up on a leash, firmly tethered by the hands of their owners. Sometimes you can trust humans to spoil the fun.

Dog is supposed to be man's best friend, if that's the case, man takes his best friend out drinking, plays cards together, will watch sporting events in bars, will ask his best friend to be best man at his wedding, but I never get taken on these jaunts. How is it then I am man's best friend?

At some point everyday, I take one of my toys to them, hoping they will engage in a tug of war, knowing my teeth are probably stronger than their grip. almost always oblige, and usually give up after I have tired them out, I hope they know how grateful I am for these little daily interludes.

Perhaps this is why, I love them, and ask little of them.

Chapter 16

SQUEALING LEFTOVERS

Mr. Bonzo may well be a prime example of how humans can get through their daily routines without too much excitement and yet when it comes to their favorite sports team, like the most mild mannered of people, he and most of the species can go berserk when their team win the World Series, triumph in a Championship game or beat bitter rivals in College Football.

Men and women whose image through their careers, can exude quiet confidence and professionalism can suddenly turn into excitable frenetic individuals, shouting, screaming, and generally reminding one of uncivilized Tribal Dancers, whether at a sports arena or in a crowd of their peers at a bar, their behavior is similar. Now if these people duplicated this activity in their offices and work places, they probably would be ostracized as lunatics and be carted off to an asylum.

However strange as this might seem, these are the same people who will scold their pet dog for jumping up and down, rolling over and over on the carpet, lying on their back with their legs in the air, and profusely enjoying themselves.

It should be stated that Mrs. Bonzo would not engage in any such activity.

Mr. Bonzo characterizes all that's wrong with the man and dog arrangement, that evokes that age old saying 'Do as I say, not necessarily as I do.' His excitement is for football, not the American variety, of padding, helmets and oxygen every five yards of running, but what the world calls football, and the United States calls soccer. From early childhood, he has followed his favorite team, in England,

and their fortunes with a passion that only a true football fan can understand, and Mrs. Bonzo can't.

He watches on them on TV, and it should come as no surprise, turns into one of those madmen you would clearly want to avoid if you had the misfortune to confront one in a public place. A near miss, a goalmouth scramble, bad foul or a goal, can send him into a jumping maniac, in concert with language one wouldn't want to repeat. Now should I jump up and down, as if a frenzied chimpanzee, I am considered naughty, but he can oblige himself during the passion of the game, without reproach.

Mrs. Bonzo has little time for sports, and less time for jumping maniacs, either of us.

I have tried soothing him at times when the language might suit something you would hear from a drunken sailor, and normal people wouldn't want to hear, and when his tantrums have become unbearable to me, I have plopped myself on his ottoman and demanded my back be rubbed. This I used to consider a dangerous move, that could cause confrontation, and took a lot of courage, but Football Maniac" does oblige, and calms down.

One time however while receiving one of the better massages I have experienced, his team scored, and all hell broke loose, as I was hoisted in the air, smothered with hugs and kisses and decidedly roughed up. was a moment that reminded me to stay away from football fans when they are watching a game and retreat to a quiet corner of the room.

So, these kind of experiences got me to thinking, how can I catch this kind of excitement? What would generate the passion, should I become a football fan, follow another sport, or take Mrs. Bonzo's advice and get interested in designer clothes and jewelry? Up to now prickly hedges and doggie treats have done the trick, but I crave more.

Speed has often been considered an aphrodisiac, and I have at times stuck my head out of the car window, with the idea that the blowing in my hair, and the feel of all that fresh air, would give me a rush. The first time I tried this, I felt no excitement at all, but that may be due to my being left in the car alone, as it was parked outside Starbucks.

ZAK

The days I am taken for a grooming, are always days to which I look forward with pleasure. With the Bonzos in tow, I usually make a mad dash through the front door of the grooming parlor, knock over anyone in sight, and scamper up to the counter with my paws resting on it, in preparation to sign the consent form. Sometimes I just can't wait for a bath.

The handlers often take their time with me, and lather me with great gusto, but it is not like soaking in a tub, with soft music, candles, and sipping an austere Chardonnay, as if an exotic love potion. I suggested this one time, but the lady who bathes me, gave me an austere look of her own, and mentioned something about an operation. Mr. Bonzo has heard Mrs. Bonzo mention this to him before now.

It's hard to imagine what it must be like if a predator, in the throws of the thrill of the chase, it is not something I do, but one time Mrs. Bonzo saw a rodent in the garden and dispatched Mr. Bonzo to, as she put it "Do something."

Armed with a pooper scooper the nearest object he could find he went into battle, with me as his lieutenant not far behind. He cornered an unfortunate small rodent, that literally had fallen from the roof, and perhaps gave new meaning to the term rat droppings, knocked it unconscious seemingly, with several swings. He also missed the target a few times, and was left somewhat embarrassed when he realized their was still "Stuff" left on the scooper from the previous day, and it flew at an exciting pace over the wall into a neighbor's garden umbrella, and left a nasty stain on an otherwise bright, cheerful and cordial tea party next door.

Their pet Shitzu who I have never had much time for, simply because he is one of those small legged varieties, and a breed that in my opinion does not have the panache afforded Wheaten Terriers, barked loudly, at least as loudly as he could, indeed it was more like a minor shriek, and generally made a nuisance of himself. I retreated back into the living room with embarrassment, but as is always the case with me, I have to go back out again just to see what's afoot.

I returned only to find Mr. Bonzo had decided to scoop some more and was filling a bag with my "Leftovers. It gave me quite shock when I perceived something inside the bag was moving, an squealing. My "Leftovers" had never done this before, and it was severe shock to the system. My suspicion was that I had contracte some rare disease, or was encountering some change in life, how could my "Stuff" squirm and squeal?

Occasionally I have noticed a rabbit wander through the garden, leaving his own leftovers, very small and not the kind of stuff I can produce. Animals with long ears should be able to do better than that.

Mr. Bonzo was holding the bag aloft it would seem with some satisfaction, and was quite taken aback with the expression on my face that must have declared consternation. The kind of look you have when you stub your toe, and await the pain.

"Got it" he declared, with a wry smile. Got what I thought, he does this everyday, when he cleans up the mess. Doesn't he know, my plight, I have squealing leftovers!

There was just a moments silence, as he walked toward the trash cans, before he let forth the most alarming shriek, after he had tripped on a garden chair and sauntered into a small prickly palm tree only a few feet in height, but with a sting a bee could produce. He started jumping up and down, and the profanity was clear for all to hear, including the neighbors, who by now had themselves retreated from their yard to a safer haven, Shitzu in tow.

Immediately I thought his team had scored a goal again, or one against them, or perhaps a penalty was awarded. How am I supposed to know the difference.

During his self inflicted melee, the bag he was holding split, and out jumped a dazed and extremely confused baby rat. Based on its appearance and intolerable odor, at first glance, I could not differentiate this pesky little animal from any other but surmised it's probably a small Chinese Water Dog.

It scampered in an Easterly direction, and burrowed under the fence into the garden next door. It didn't take long for screams to be forthcoming, and shrieks of a loud nature, from generally mild mannered neighbors. Maybe their team scored a goal I thought.

Mr. Bonzo put what was left in the bag, into the trash can, and beat a hasty retreat inside the house. I quickly followed having rendered as much aide as I was going to for that day. Mrs. Bonzo inquired as to what all the noise was about, as she lay prostrate on the sofa, filing her nails, and wrapped in a bath towel looking calmly serene, and with a perfumed air about her.

"Nothing dear," replied a limping, but near conquering Mr. Bonzo, all I could think of, was simply Shitzu happens.

Chapter 17

THEY CALL IT A VACATION

The Bonzos left me at the vet, on their way to the airport, as they started on their trip to Europe. Not for the first time they led me like a horse to water, carrying a little bag with some treats and a few of my favorite toys.

My stay is something I can never figure out, how long will it be?

When I'm taken to this boarding house, I can't tell if it's just for a bath, some check up or other, or a prolonged stay. There's no way I can know on entry, so as is my usual custom I just race through the front door, with little expectations.

The Bonzos on the other hand, stay in posh hotels, dine in fine restaurants, and generally pamper themselves. I get one meal a day, lie in a cramped cage, and am completely bored. Luckily I get taken out for a walk twice a day, or I would go stir crazy. Yet when they pick me up after their vacation is over, I am supposed to greet them as though I have had such a good time, and should be so grateful I wasn't left on my own at home, or with strangers. Don't they realize they leave me with strangers at the vet.

Airports according to Mr. Bonzo, particularly international airports should insist passengers dress according to the tradition of the country to which they are traveling. For example men going to Vienna should wear Lederhosen, women Heidi type outfits, going to Bejing, Chinese Kaftans, this would make life much easier for airline staff to recognize where everyone is traveling to, and would never have to ask at the ticket counter as to their destination. Mrs. Bonzo has difficulty when flying into an airport, she gets nervous hearing airline flight attendants use the word 'terminal.'

Mr. Bonzo has his own ideas on flying, he told me once he cannot understand why flight attendants, always state they are there primarily for the passengers safety. "It's just a disguise so they shouldn't be considered flying waitresses, why is it Zak if that's the case, you never see them checking the aircraft before take off." He rambled on with "They don't fill up the plane with fuel, and I have never seen them make sure the toilets are working properly."

"Always check the height of your pilot" said Mrs Bonzo, as they waited for their flight to depart. "In the Air Force pilots can only be a certain height" she continued.

Considering this to be a typical Mrs. Bonzo "Incoming" Mr. Bonzo politely declined to comment at that time, except a moment later a rather tall pilot passed by.

"It's probably why they have that bubble on the top of a 747, for tall pilots" he retorted.

The Bonzos were on their way to Europe for a mini vacation, which meant, I was going to be stuck at the vet's in a cage for ten days, or to put it succinctly in a room with no view. If I had my way I'd like a large room with bath and shower, mini bar and room service, preferably at the Ritz.

Evidently they set off on their adventures without a care in the world, while I relived my days in the pet shop where once a long time ago, I was confined while on sale. Isn't it funny how some things come back to haunt you.

So it seems that on this trip for the Bonzos history repeated itself, and they were once again faced with what was for them, the daunting task of trying to exit a parking garage in a foreign country. Some two years before my arrival, they spent a week in the South of France, mostly touring with Mr. Bonzo driving and Mrs. Bonzo navigator in chief, a position she never asked for, and which rarely merits high marks from Mr. Bonzo. normally get lost at least once an hour.

You know how when you ask for directions from someone, they always seem to be a stranger to the area, Mrs. Bonzo claims she's a stranger to a map. She really does find it easier to turn a map upside down when traveling south.

They came across a small town somewhere in Provence, which happened to be market day. With no parking in sight Mr. Bonzo spotted a sign in French stating "Parking" it was simply the letter P, and since Mr. Bonzo considers himself something of a linguist, he decided this meant parking. So with much aplomb he entered, taking a ticket as the barrier went up, found a space to park and readied themselves for the jaunt ahead. It was on their return that the trouble started.

Reversing out of the parking space, they looked for the exit' which in French of course is 'Sortie.' Once they found it they drove in circles up the ramp until they encountered an attendant seated in his an enclosed glass cage. "Monsieur, combien" asked Mr. Bonzo in best French accent. Ibe stoic attendant did nothing other than point his finger upwards, so the Bonzos drove round and round the ramp upwards until they encountered another sign 'Sortie' it declared. Following the signs to the letter of the law, they arrived at the same glass window with the same stoic attendant, who once again pointed his finger upward. Once again they circled via the ramps, and once again they ended up with the stoic attendant who for the third time pointed his finger in an upward direction.

With frustration setting in, Mr Bonzo did the same only the intent behind it was not in a kindly manner. He stepped out of the car and addressed Monsieur Stoic. "Monsieur" he said, "How do I get out." Ihe Frenchman once again pointed upward, but this time spoke in rapid southern French style. Mr. Bonzo understood none of it. Magically the attendant held out his hand as if to receive money, and the Bonzos paid him. It was only on their exit they realized up on the top floor was a machine where you could purchase a ticket to insert in a slot next to the exit barrier, that would lift and let them out, and it was to this the attendant was referring.

On this current vacation in Paris, they rented a car at Hertz, where the rental car had to be picked up seven floors below sea level and in a very dark atmosphere. After crashing the gears several times, the car was not an automatic, and navigating the upward spiral about as wide as the car itself, they faced a closed garage door. It was the kind of door that requires an opener, found in millions of homes, but, not what you might expect after an uphill spiral, that resembled the Leaning Tower of Pisa. On facing the door, the Bonzos were perplexed.

"There must be a button to push" pronounced Mrs. Bonzo, which was greeted with much discontent from her husband. "I suppose you would like me to ask for directions" he retorted.

At that moment, Mr. Bonzo spied two things, a notice in English and French clearly advocating Let incoming cars enter first' he opted to read that in English, and a button on the wall which looked like it needed to be pushed to raise the garage door. Since the width of the path was no more than six inches beyond the width of the car, and that made it impossible to open the car door, he leaned out of the window of the small compact French car, and was just about able to reach within two feet of the button. Stepping on the drivers seat with his upper torso out of the window, where he was in no mans land outside the car. He was stuck in the open car window, just as another rental car drove up behind him. Not able to turn in his current position he couldn't tell who was behind him, but did manage to 'Push the button". As if by magic, up went the door, and daylight fell upon them.

Unfortunately, facing them was a small truck the kind you might see delivering cheese and wine to flea markets, although I didn't know fleas consumed cheese and wine, perhaps French fleas do. On the drivers side sat a portly man wearing a the Gaelic equivalent of a baseball cap, with the words "Fromage et Vin, Viva La France" clearly visible.

On seeing the garage door open, he engaged gears to move forward, he also pointed upward to the sign that Mr. Bonzo had previously read in his fluent English 'Let incoming cars enter first'.

Having managed to seat himself again, he arrived in the driving position to witness Mrs. Bonzo put up her hand as if a policeman stopping traffic, and in his rear view mirror a Swiss tourist honking his horn.

The horn a long Alpenhorn usually seen in Alpine villages, blown by men in lederhosen and feathered hats, to attract tourists, was situated on the roof, the large end facing the rear, and the driver leaning out of his driver's side window, seemingly stuck in his compact French car, blowing as hard as he could.

Mr. Bonzo waved to the Frenchman to retreat, into the street behind him, which was as is typical in small Parisian streets full of traffic, with pedestrians arguing about who had the right of way. Once again the Frenchman pointed his finger upward toward the sign.

"Go back" shouted the Bonzos, and with that the Swiss Alpenhorn blower retreated, with what sounded like excerpts from the Sound of Music, ringing through underground. The message was intended for the vehicle ahead of them, and after a stand off that lasted a few minutes, the Frenchman backed out into the street, and graciously allowed the Bonzos space to exit. Unfortunately for the truck driver, as the Bonzos sped away, the garage door closed leaving him once again waiting for someone to open the door from the inside.

"Sacre bleu" could be heard faintly in the distance, along with an occasional oomp pah pah, from beneath the streets.

When people stay in a hotel room they are away from the rest of humanity, when animals are boarded, the cages are all in a row, and day or night, weird noises can be heard from adjoining cages, or one that is further along cell block 29. Bulldogs for example have a wind problem, at their rear end, small dogs tend to yap and squeak, at a time I am usually trying to sleep, and with all this in mind, they call it a vacation.

Chapter 18

KEYS IN THE SONG OF LIFE

Mr Bonzo is not an accomplished musician, but he plays piano with a passion and abandonment and while doing so, I lay on the floor next to him, sometimes wishing I had longer ears, like a cocker spaniel, the type that could block out sounds when you don't want hear something. His repertoire stretches from pop to classical, and Mrs. Bonzo listens while cooking in the kitchen, I try not to, since he never plays my favorites, and frankly isn't that good, thankfully he doesn't play the tuba.

Sometimes I wish I knew the title of what he is playing, some times he tells me, and one time it got me thinking how appropriate it would be if song titles matched the mood I'm in, or memories that come to mind.

For example 'Never on Sunday' would be good, when on Sunday's we never seem to do much. Just for listening to his playing "'What Kind of Fool am I'" would suit, although Mrs. Bonzo would argue Don't Bring Me Flowers" as appropriate as you can get. She is a wonderful cook, dinner guests leave in raptures after a feast. I always get little pieces of chicken if I sit nicely by the side of her, with an adoring look on my face, but never sample fettuccine Alfredo or a seared ahi tuna, in a white wine sauce.

Just waiting with an air of expectation for a little treat can be

described as a 'Let it Be Me', just seeing the look on Mr. Bonzo's

face as he plays something he really likes, with me by his side, ergo...

'As Long as He Needs Me'. For my stuffed toy dog called Madeleine who I have come to adore "Don't Know Much" and if

I ever get an answer to the notice posted at the vet, for female companionship, I would like to have placed, "I Finally Found Someone."

When given the opportunity to roam free in the woods without a leash "Unchained Melody" fits the bill. If you have a pet of your own, just take a good look at your precious one and see which song would be suitable in their eyes, you might be surprised.

For the dogs I meet on our jaunts through the neighborhood for the most part " "Go Your Own Way" I deem appropriate. After a trip for a check up at the vet "My Heart Will Go On" and no one would argue with me that for the Bonzos I can categorically state my wish for them would be "I'll Be There."

One day Mr. Bonzo played only classical music, some of his beloved Bach, and Beethoven, which is very difficult to match with events or things that happen in my life. After all, what can I equate with the "Little Fugue in G Minor" other than that infernal Shitzu I hear yapping from time to time, or the "Piano Sonata Pathetique" which might reflect how many hear his piano playing.

Hell hath no fury like a woman scorned, never merits Mrs. Bonzo's mood but could earn distinction if the pianist played Mozart's Queen of the Nights Vengeance" aria from the Magic Flute.

As Shakespeare put it 'If music be the food of love, play 0m, but I'd rather let a nice piece of chicken breast take preference with music playing on. Music is always in abundance in our household the radio, CD's mostly classical, as Mrs. Bonzo says when there is a silence, without the tender background of Brahms or Chopin C' It's like an old peoples home in here", don't they know they are old people, I am living in an old peoples home!

It is certainly pleasurable to smell the fine aroma from the kitchen, as Mrs. Bonzo prepares the next meal, with tender music in the background, many times I just lay nonchalantly on the carpet, careful to avoid pet stains, and sometimes simply doze off, or think silly thoughts.

For example when an army marches into a foreign country, such as the Germans did in the second World War, and through a strange town, how did they know where to go. Old newsreels show them marching toward City Hall or Government buildings, but there was no one at the front with a map shouting "Turn left at Main Street chaps, then right at the High Street" at least as far as I can tell.

When the Romans conquered Britain, did they ask for directions at the nearest pub? Of course Hannibal crossing the Alps would not have had anyone to ask, he was probably up to his knees in snow.

Music has always been a part of stirring men into battle, or the general population into National pride. In America "The Star Mangled Banger" brings tears to the eyes of a rowdy crowd at the Super Bowl, or the college campus at graduation, "Land of Hope and Glory" or as it is sometimes called "The Pompous Circus Dance will be remembered by graduating students forever. In Britain "For God's sake save us from the Queen" can easily turn most, into tears.

Sometimes it occurs to me, especially when Mr. Bonzo hits a wrong note, what if the lyrics were changed in movie musicals, would people still have fond memories of Julie Andrews in the Sound of Music if she sang " hills are alive with the sound of flatulence" or in the final scene of Carousel, Gordon McCrae sang "When you walk through a cow pat" instead of through a storm, no doubt he would still have kept his head up high.

On one of my snoozing adventures as I like to call them, I considered famous men, and what if their speeches were altered just a little, such as Roosevelt, with a vivid imagination can't you see him saying "The only thing we have to fear, is a dental hygienist"

Churchill's infamous wartime speech "Give us the tools and we will all become handymen" could also come to mind.

For a wheaten like me, just the jingle of car keys makes me jump with delight at the thought ofan outing, wherever I may go, they are "Keys to the Throng of Life."

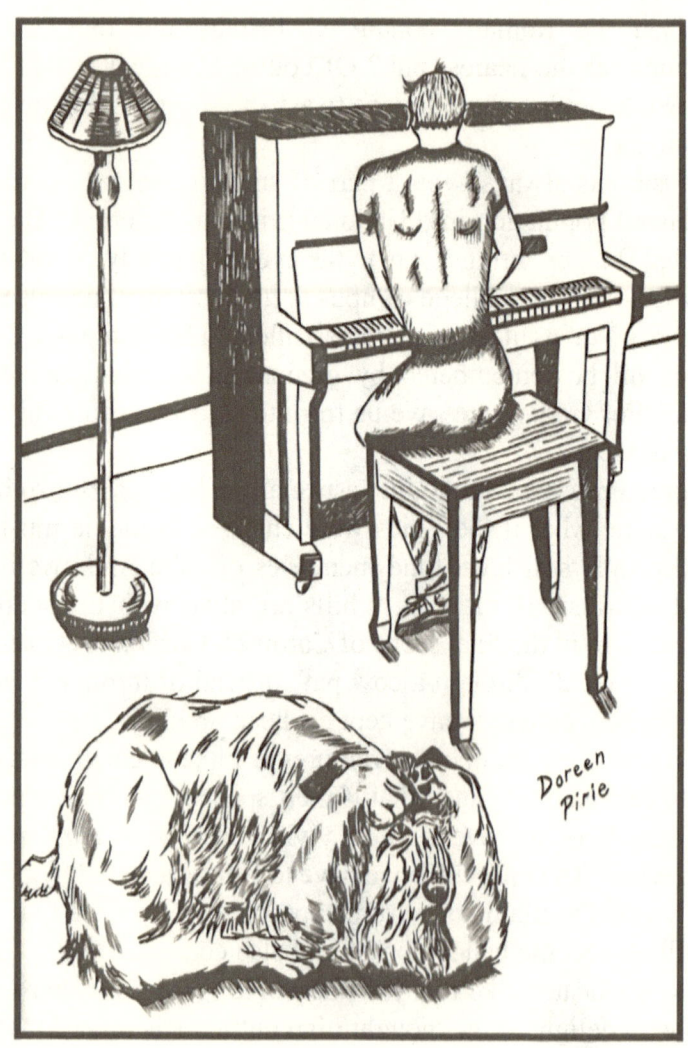

Chapter 19

CAN'T SEE THE WOODS FOR THE TREES

Is there anything more exciting than a trip to the woods, to roam free among the trees and pathways, with small twigs stuck in my fur, and mud up my legs, attracting tics and fleas, just after being groomed, and fit for a photo op.

Occasionally I do get tics and fleas, and one time after a bath the grooming lady pronounced she had found one tic. Now I ask you, the indignity of it, is one thing, but how can you find just one tic or one flea, unless at a flea circus perhaps.

Once in a while the Bonzos take me to a nearby National Park intended to afford me exercise, and often resulting in their frustration at my muddy paws. It is not unknown to bounce back into the car after such an expedition with a dozen small branches wrapped around, exhausted, in search of a rest, and that's just typical of the Bonzos.

I certainly need the activity, and obviously they do, as they trudge wearily back to the car, with a smile on their faces claiming how invigorating it all was. Sometimes they just can't see the woods for the trees.

On a regular basis, our cleaning Lady whom I shall call Eva came every week, and regular as clockwork, every week the Bonzos search the house for items Eva has put away, but they can't find. Eva is a dear Mexican lady whose English extends to "Puppy" when she addresses me, but speaks in Spanish for just about everything else. Occasionally she will address me in her native tongue with 'Cacharro' the Spanish for Puppy, I simply refuse to respond under such circumstances, I much prefer 'Cuco' which of course means cute, it sounds better and much more appropriate.

Eva would change the contents of the cupboards on a regular basis, so that when the Bonzos open them up to get a cup or dinners plates, they are just not where they thought they should be. I am eternally grateful to Eva for never changing the spot where my treats reside, I always know where to find them, the Bonzos are not so fortunate.

Dubbed the 'Case of the Missing Duvet' one time they searched frantically for a bed cover in all nooks and crannies of the house, without success, and this after taking one off the bed and shipping it to the cleaners. The search lasted days, and surprisingly neither the FBI or the CIA was called in. With all the commotion generated between husband and wife over missing bed linen, you would have thought a family heirloom was lost, or a National Treasure had been absconded. Several calls to Eva resulted in the possibility by her account, that the last time it was taken to the cleaners it was never returned.

Since I accompany Mr. Bonzo every week on the cleaning run I can attest I never did see it come back, but nobody consults or takes any notice of me when a Red Alert is in force.

According to Mrs. Bonzo that's not the only thing that recently disappeared. One day standing in the doorway to the music room, aka the study, Mrs Bonzo surprised Mr. Bonzo and me draped in a bathing suit with a bold statement "My Kaplotza's disappeared."

For all you language aficionados, I'm not sure you'll recognize the word Kaplotza, some call it a derriere, others rear end, many just plain bottom.

Mr. Bonzo and I were stunned, it was not that it was an unannounced incoming, so much as a statement received with disbelief. I had never seen Mrs. Bonzo in a bathing suit before, so for me it was a double whammy, Mr. Bonzo stared vacantly into space, as Mrs. Bonzo turned round to display all her curves but little left in the Kaplotza area. As you might imagine, she was not too happy with herself, although comforted by Mr. Bonzo, she was resolute in her unhappiness to think one part of her anatomy was not what it used to be.

Mr. Bonzo loves her just the way she is, but she thinks, this will make a difference, sometimes she can't see the woods for trees.

IF ONLY I COULD TELL THEM

Duvets and Kaplotzas are not the only thing that has been MIA, One time they couldn't find my large bag of dog food, usually stored in the garage, out of Eva's reach or so they thought. As I sat patiently in the kitchen with that hungry look on my face, I have nearly perfected that now, they turned the garage upside down, like an ATF raid on a narcotics house, looking for evidence.

One hour later they discovered a rotund box that contained all the hard bits that make dinner appetizing for me, Eva had emptied the contents of the bag into the box that has a sealed lid, to keep the contents fresh. It made sense, but the Bonzos were not amused at another necessary hunt and quickly ran to the pantry, to make sure all the contents were still there, instead of the bathroom, or a bedroom or wherever else La Senora decided they should go.

You would think after years of these episodes, the Bonzos would confront Eva, and once they did.

"Eva" said Mrs. Bonzo nonchalantly "You come very week, and each time you hide everything we're looking for, please leave everything where it is."

"Si" replied Eva.

"You understand?" inquired Mrs. Bonzo.

"Good" responded Mrs. Bonzo.

"Que" said Eva.

"You do understand don't you?" inquired Mrs. Bonzo once again.

"Si" was the response. "Puppy good" she went on.

"No, Eva."

"Puppy not good?" asked Eva, with the beginnings of a sad face about to emerge.

"No, don't hide things so we can't find them" a frustrated Mrs. Bonzo retorted.

"Me hide Puppy?" suggested Eva.

"No Eva, do not hide puppy, do not hide anything" once again Mrs. Bonzo showing signs of strain.

Eva then went into a stunning array of Spanish, lasting at least five minutes presumably on the merits of not hiding puppy, the good and bad news about Tacos, her cousin is visiting from Mexico City and for all we know global warming, at the end of which however all one could discern was, "Me not hide puppy.

81

Enter into the affray Mr. Bonzo, who had just discovered of his tools were missing, this was a surprise, since Mr. Bonzo is not really a handyman, and rarely visits his toolbox. In fact, we believe his last time handling a hammer or wrench was during the Nixon administration. However, at that very moment it seemed he had the desire the fix a leaky faucet.

"Eva, have you seen my wrench" he asked politely,

"You have a wench" suggested Eva, at which point Mrs. Bonzo gave him a look, that suggested a guillotine may be her next purchase.

"No, no, Eva wrench, not wench" he protested.

"I not speak with men who have wenches" Eva said, stamping her foot, impatiently, and seemingly about to launch into fandango.

"Eva" Mr Bonzo went on "Eva, by the way why is it we can't find anything after you have cleaned up."

"Me not hide Puppy" was her response.

A bewildered Mr. Bonzo, not a party to the previous discussions, shook his head, and departed in search of his wench.

Calmly I had sat in the kitchen facing the two women reminiscent of dueling banjos, motionless, quiet and extremely patient. As always in these circumstances I am given the deep freeze, as if still in the Ice Age, completely frozen out, suddenly I let out the most discerning bark I could muster, partly to attract attention, and partly because I thought it might be time for dinner. Upon which Eva proclaimed and it appeared with some satisfaction "See I not hide Puppy."

Sometimes they just can't perceive the words for the freeze.

Chapter 20

WHAT DO THEY DO IN THERE

So many times I am left wondering, as I sit patiently in the car, when they trot off to places unknown. As I sit watching the world go by and left to view humanity in all its glory, what are they doing in there.

Parking lots can be interesting places, have you ever-questioned human behavior, as a non member myself, I often speculate why for example some humans return shopping carts to their rightful place at supermarket parking stalls, while others just leave them abandoned in different directions for someone else to collect, and some let them roll around on their own, to land wherever they may. I can remember watching one take on a life of its own, as it rolled on a slight incline, between parked cars, and passing vehicles to end up just next to a dumpster, and not one human tried to stop it, bet this wouldn't happen if it was a baby carriage.

Some people return to their cars with hoards of paper or plastic bags, some just one bag, it seems the older people are, the less bags they carry. Bonzos should carry one bag between them.

Then there is the array of humans departing from the store, different shapes and sizes, mostly wearing blue jeans, which amazes me, why don't jeans come in as many colors as pants? Trousers as Mr. Bonzo describes them, can be spotted in so many different colors, yet jeans are always blue.

Why aren't humans categorized the same way as dogs, by breed? Surely if the human race can come up with breeds for dogs, they can do it for themselves. Take for example small children always into something, couldn't they be terriers, those snoozing in their arm chairs, with the occasional wind, bulldogs, and young men in search of a girl friend could be the 'Hunting Group" and it doesn't take much to recognize the larger form of humans on their way back to parked vehicles, slowly carrying enormous quantities of food and drink as would St. Bernards.

I rarely see other dogs sitting patiently in parked vehicles, they are either yapping at passers by, or looking out for their owners. I do this, and sometimes I just wish I had binoculars, the Bonzos always seem to park so far away from their destination. With binoculars I would also have the chance to see what it is they do in the places they visit.

It's easy to think for oneself viewing all around you from a parked car, and with time on your paws, so it came to mind one day, why do all these cars look alike? If humans and dogs are so different to one another, why should cars not be as different as the human race. Perhaps they are all designed by "General" Motors.

The Bonzos often return to the car, exhausted after a trip to the market, and based on the discussion when they get into the car I think every now and then I understand. The weekly trip to the market can evoke emotions beyond my comprehension. Even stowing the groceries in the car can start a confrontation, "Put them here, put them there" I hear followed by "Be careful with this" or don't put that on top of something or other, then we drive off to the sound of clanking noises, and items spilling in different directions, from the rear of the car, like the shopping carts in the parking lot.

Mr. Bonzo complains about how long he has to wait while she stands and stares at the shelves, the same ones every week, with the same items on them, nothing is changed, except when the day comes the market manager has decided to move the stuff to different aisles, and humanity rises as if going to war, in order to complain to any market staff in earshot, a difficult thing to do, since market staff a rarely seen when needed, let alone in earshot.

If Mr. Bonzo picks an item Mrs. Bonzo has to inspect it to make sure it is what's needed, yet when she has forgotten something, and dispatches Mr. Bonzo to another aisle to get it, it's perfectly OK no matter what he comes back with, go figure.

IF ONLY I COULD TELL THEM

Then there's the coupons that they take, and there are multitudes of them, and maybe they will use a couple at the check out counter, Mrs. Bonzo sits at the table every Sunday morning clipping them from the paper, and occasionally remembers to take them with on the jaunt, only to find by the time she does remember to take them, many of them are out of date, the thought often occurs to me, did they buy me with coupons, and how many did it take? If they did' they could not have been beyond the sell by time, because so often good things don't have an expiration date.

I never get left in the car for very long, mostly because anything from the market that has the opportunity to melt means I am not going to be left for long, but if they are going to be any length Of time, I don't get to go.

At home, both of them disappear into the bathroom and close the door, not at the same time I should add, what do they do behind dosed doors? For the most part, Mr. Bonzo is in and out in a minute, just occasionally longer, Mrs. Bonzo stays forever, and always after they emerge, I hear the noise of flushing water, yet when the faucet in the kitchen is running, the noise is the same but there are no closed doors, similarly when they water the garden with a hose, all the doors are open. One day I'll find out what they do in there.

I never get the chance to go behind closed doors, and do anything I want, if that were to happen, and I could not be found, they would send out a search and rescue team for me, probably complete with helicopters and two USAF F16's.

Very occasionally the Bonzos disappear in to the garage, and I hear rumbling, noises suggesting items being moved, or a general cleaning out, and I am never invited to participate. What do they do in there?

Having now established myself as a fully grown Wheaten, you would think I would be privy to the events behind closed doors, or in places I have yet to visit, probably on account of inexperience. Life for a Wheaten can be hard if not exposed to all the world can offer, will they never take me in there with them.

Chapter 21

ZIPPER DE DOO DAI-I

I always cherish those times I cuddle up to Mrs. Bonzo, and she pets me lovingly, as if nothing changed from the first time I set eyes on her, as a very young puppy, imprisoned in a pet shop, and she asked Mr. Bonzo if they were going to take me home.

After a hard day, doing whatever she does, and that still remains a mystery to me, a few minutes together in an embrace on the sofa, or flat on the living room floor, with love abounding makes the day worthwhile. Mr. Bonzo pets me often as well, but I am always swayed by her gentle touch and those little words of affection, she offers every now and again that make me feel good. Together on her chair there is no height differential, makes me feel as if I'm an equal' unlike staring up at either of them when I am on all fours.

Small animals have a distinct disadvantage, even standing for example when it starts to rain, together with dwarfs and midgets we are among the last to know. I don't like rain, it ruins my garden routines, I have come to the conclusion the little pitter patter of raindrops, is a signal for me not venture outside.

As' you can tell, I often listen to the Bonzos and their stories of bygone days, and while receiving an intoxicating cuddle, one day overheard them giggling over the time they went to the ballet, and Mr. Bonzo's zipper got stuck.

It would seem, on the way to the performance his shirt popped out, through an unsuspecting opening in his pants, while leisurely strolling to the theatre, arm in arm with his wife, dressed to the nines. It's odd to think one's zipper can unsettle itself at moments like that.

"Don't worry" said Mrs. Bonzo to a somewhat grumpy husband.

"What do you mean don't worry, my shirt is poking out of my pants, and I can't stuff it back in, every time I try, it just pops out again" responded Mr. Grumpy.

"No one will see" came the reply.

As they entered the foyer, and through the milling throng, Mr. Bonzo seemed ill at ease with his plight, but Mrs. Bonzo stayed close to him and half a pace in front, to hide any possible embarrassment as they headed in the direction of the bar.

"What would you like to drink" offered Mr. Bonzo

"I'll have a shirt, I mean short drink" she said.

He trotted off to the bartender, retrieved two glasses and rejoined Mrs. Bonzo. As they chatted about the upcoming event they were to see, the Nutcracker, suddenly Mr. Bonzo was bumped from behind and as one can be, in crowded bars, he turned around to be confronted by a dwarf, whose eyes were directly in line with his forlorn zipper, and sparkling white shirt front, protruding from a wide open vent.

Neither Mr. Bonzo or the dwarf were expecting such a sight, not on the opening night of the Nutcracker, and both let out a scream of surprise. Naturally this attracted much attention from the milling throng who had gravitated from the foyer to the bar, and were witnessing an unusual situation. I know how the dwarf must have felt, when you are at a low height, you see things in a different pespective.

Mr. Bonzo turned to Mrs. Bonzo, his now smiling companion, and said "I thought you said no one will see."

"Well there's not very much to see" quoted Mrs. Bonzo.

"Depends on your height" came a quick retort.

Worse was to follow as they took their seats, which happened to be at the end of the row, as they sat down his shirt became even more visible popping out upward from of the vent, and being at the end of the row as patrons arrived he had to rise to let them by. Each time theatre goers sidled by, they would seem to focus on his lap, and each time Mrs. Bonzo would have to comfort her husband without "No one will see."

ZAK

As you might have expected the last of the patrons to take their seats, did not require anyone to rise, to let them by, it was of course the dwarf. He could have sprinted through the row without disturbing a soul, yet on arrival at Row 12, he stood motionless as he eyed Mr. Bonzo, before inching past him. Not a word was spoken between them, but a long blank glare told it's own story.

It suddenly occurred to me, that when people attempt to up smoking, many try using what is known as the patch. According to the instructions on many brands, you have to place it above (he waist, on a non hairy part, and each day place a new one on skin has not had a patch before, for several weeks. Probably most people run out of places to put them, but what does a smoking dwarf do? I mean he doesn't have a lot of room, does he?

I never found out the end of that story, as often happens I dozed off content with the thought that the embraceable Mrs Bonzo has me locked in a cuddle, caressing me, although I vaguely remember something about a police station, and a dwarf with a black eye, while Mr. Bonzo snored ungraciously having missed another of his favorite programs on TV due to the days battle fatigue.

I feel so much better when I am on the same level, nodding off, with the strains of Zipper De Doo Dah in my head.

Chapter 22

FEELING BLUE

I have been told many times, as has the Bonzos, mostly by strangers, that I am a happy dog. How do they know, what symptoms do I display to give them encouragement to have that thought. Don't they know I have mood swings too, some times I just feel blue, sometimes I feel happy in the morning and blue in the afternoon, even depressed by dinner time.

Best of all, it's my call how I feel, unless depressive thoughts abound, or I just don't feel too good, it got me to considering, what makes me that way.

First off, if bored by lack of activity or the prickly hedges have been over trimmed by the gardeners, leaving the itch factor decidedly non existent, it can make me dull, as at a very early age I lost my jewels. This obviously leads to a sense of foreboding continuing on to semi-blue days. I tend under such circumstances to lay around my head on my paws, trying to think of something exciting to plan to get me back to happy paws conditioning.

On one such occasion as I lay in the kitchen watching the Bonzos read their Sunday paper, coffee cups brimming with activity, Mrs. Bonzo reading the opinion section, quite apropos, she always has Mr. Bonzo in a brain consuming crossword mode, a ritual that one, requires much concentration and some brain power, I'm not sure he has either, it was such a day that I realized humans too can have days of the blues.

If the opinion doesn't meet Mrs. Bonzo's standards or the crossword proves to be too difficult, or on rare moment of panic Mr. Bonzo asks her for help on a clue, to which if the reply he gets doesn't meet required standards, the air can be filled with a silence all of its own.

For example, as I lay unnoticed under the kitchen table, not an easy thing to accomplish, to be unnoticed, I mean, the table is glass, surely they can see me through it, you will not be surprised by now to hear the following banter occurred as I recall on what I labeled 'Blue Sunday'.

Mr. Bonzo "Four letter word for 'to egg on.

Mrs. Bonzo "Toast."

"Toast, that's five letters" retorted Mr. Bonzo.

"Well I can't help it if the word has too many letters" she replied.

Which letter do you think is in there, that shouldn't be?" inquired Mr. Bonzo.

"T" she stated emphatically.

Which one?" he asked one eye raised in disbelieE

Your choice" she giggled.

"Sometimes I just get an urge, when you are in this mood to ignore you" he stated.

"There you are then, 'to egg on' four letters... Urge, see you can't complete the crossword without me" smirked Mrs. Bonzo.

For a few minutes there was silence, it would seem the article in the paper, Mrs. Bonzo was quietly reading, was on tax deductions and in a typical Mrs. Bonzo moment, when calm seemed to be restored, and all about us was serene, she offered, "Why can't we take Zak as a deduction?

Now you need to understand Mr. Bonzo had absolutely no clue at that moment what she was reading, and for that matter neither did I, but on hearing my name called, naturally I rose from the floor, looked up expecting a treat or a pat on the head, or a signal that we were to depart for a walk, although the last thought was merely wishful thinking, since neither of them were appropriately attired for a walk, or much else, as they were both in their pajamas.

Mr Bonzo clearly getting aggravated responded with "Deduct Zak from what?" "Our tax return" she replied.

"Don't be silly" he said, and with that, the banter continued., until both tired of the subject matter.

My thoughts on this were however, ongoing. I don't have an income, I don't pay taxes, I don't even have a social security number, other than the Bonzos who officially knows I exist. I never get mail' except for a wistful birthday card from the vet, and I am not registered to vote, all very strong reasons to feel blue.

Even if I could vote, I wouldn't know for whom, but it would be nice at least to have the opportunity. Why couldn't I run for Office' representing breeds everywhere, under the banner vote for the TFC party, which stands for "Treats for Canines.

As the morning wore on, and there was hardly a stir from those at the kitchen table, and I lay prostrate and motionless, I couldn't help feeling there must be more to life, than feeling blue and so there was. In a moment of confusion I heard them whisper to one another with obviously me as the subject. I can tell when they are talking about me, their volume goes down and they look at me furtively, the kind of look that tells you bad news is coming. They also do a lot of pointing with fingers outstretched.

It is bad enough I had to learn English, it seems I should study sign language, if I am not to be outwitted.

"He has to go on a diet" said Mr. Bonzo.

"He needs more exercise as well" Mrs. Bonzo contributed.

"The vet said he's overweight, he has to lose 1 0 lbs, we have to cut down on his treats, and buy that healthy dog food, you know the lite stuff" he whispered.

If I felt blue before this announcement, I was now downright depressed. Reducing my treats, was not good news, since these are highlights of my day. Where was Eva the housekeeper when I needed her, she could hide them, and feed me large quantities when she came to the house I thought, she wouldn't know I had to go on a diet. I snuggled in a corner, paws outstretched, to put together a game plan.

One of my greatest fears as a puppy was hearing the vet tell Mr. Bonzo a long time ago, I would grow to thirty five or forty pounds, the day had come, maybe they won't love me anymore, maybe I am too fat or overweight, just large boned I pondered to myself, or just maybe could I be in denial. No I thought that's in Egypt, denial I mean, or is it Africa. On returning to the kitchen table the Bonzos were still discussing the merits of how to perform weight reduction on me, I looked at both of them sat down, and wistfully begged for a treat, lifting my right paw in the air, and giving them my sad face to look at, in the hope they would take pity upon me. If only I could break into a song or deliver a speech that could inspire, that would move them into action. No such luck, all I got was "You are on a diet'"

I just felt like singing the blues.

Chapter 23

TRUE COLORS

Another weekend rolled around, I can tell when that happens, both the Bonzos are in the bathroom at the same time. Weekdays they fall out of bed at different times, and make there way to the bathroom more slowly.

This was different, after dressing they started to move the furniture into the garage, and take pictures off the wall. Goodness gracious are they moving somewhere? I suspected something was going to change, and suddenly felt very insecure. had talked about their dreams of one day moving to another State, possibly Connecticut or anywhere that had tall trees, four seasons and a pond. I felt this was the moment they were actually going to do it or are they in a state of confusion?

California is all I have known for the last two years, it is sunny, sometimes hot, and rarely rains, surely this suits them. What four seasons can they be looking for? Don't they know there are four seasons here, earthquakes, mudslides, brushfires and divorce.

Maybe they are splitting up, but I quickly put that out of my mind, they seem so happy together and its obvious they love each other. Maybe they really are moving. Will they take me, or leave me behind?

My insecurities surfaced more strongly, as more chairs, lamps and other artifacts they had collected over the years found their way to the garage. Just a thought, but perhaps they were hiding stuff from Eva the housekeeper, who you recall was the culprit on many occasion of changing stuff in cupboards and closets, so the Bonzos couldn't find anything. This could be their way of showing Eva whose boss.

The whole weekend saw them lifting, huffing, puffing and generally knocking themselves out, and commenting how years ago this would have been easier for them, a break in the action resulted in a candid conversation.

"It's no fun, getting old" said an exhausted Mrs. Bonzo.

I wouldn't know" responded Mr. Bonzo

"Look at you" she continued "You look like you are about to collapse."

Mr. Bonzo leaning on the kitchen counter, and sipping a cup of tea, was indeed not a pretty sight, perspiring, hair all over the place, breathing heavily and rubbing his shoulder, as if it was about to off, he could hardly stand. I hope I don't find myself like that when I get old or have to move somewhere.

"I am just taking a breather" he said.

"I am not sure how many breaths you've got left" she replied.

"The secret, my dear, to my longevity is every time I breathe out' I breathe in again" he calmly responded.

"It won't be long before we will just have the energy to get up in the morning" she went on.

"I can't wait for the day we can retire, leisurely, slowly, and gently walk hand in hand into... the pharmacy" he stated.

As the weekend came to a close, and not much was left in any room except their bed, and of course Mrs. Bonzo's make up stuff and hair spray, I snuggled into them as often as I could, to remind them I want to go with them wherever they go.

The following morning my worst fears were realized. I was dumped into the car, and unceremoniously shipped off to the vet. As Mr. Bonzo signed the necessary papers, the staff whisked me off to a cage out of sight from the main counter. Was this the last time I will see them?

A couple of days went by, and I was still caged. Ruefully I contemplated life as I would know it, since I had not been given a bath, I knew I was to be here for some time. Who would collect me, who would I live with now? Why did the Bonzos forsake me, are they showing their true colors? I had so many questions.

As time rolled by, wistfully I contemplated my future, was it to be here boarded, caged like a life sentence, was I to live somewhere else, would I always be as sad as I feel now, color me blue again.

Then a miracle happened, one afternoon probably four days or so after I entered so ruefully, I was bathed, shampooed, smelled good, and taken to the main counter, a ritual that usually takes place at a breakneck pace on my part, dragging the young lady who retrieves me, through doors and corridors, that would match an express train. This day I was faster than usual, I could have sprinted in a track race, perhaps I am getting out of here, am I going home.

On arrival in the lobby, there was Mr. Bonzo arms outstretched as usual to greet me. Did he know how happy I was to see him, could he understand my joy at that moment, life was suddenly good again. Take me home please I thought, take me home.

As we left, I sprinted once again, this time to the car, Mr Bonzo lifted me into the back seat, and mentally I broke into song "Hi Ho, Hi Ho, its off to home we go" in my head.

On arrival, there was, Mrs. Bonzo, my immortal beloved, with my dinner ready and waiting, oh it's so nice to go traveling, but so much nicer to be home. It wasn't until I had finished my meal, lapped up some water that I noticed an odd smell about the place. I ran around the house, and it didn't matter which room I entered, they all had the same odor. It was while in the Bonzo's bedroom, that it occurred to me, the walls are not the same. They used to be all white, now they have color, I quickly ran into the living room, wouldn't you know it, that was a different color, so was the music room.

It took a few moments for me to realize the furniture was back, so were the lamps, the artifacts, everything was back to normal. The house had been painted, changed from white walls to different shades, but most importantly I was home, and the Bonzos didn't move, they didn't let me go, they showed their true colors.

Chapter 24

IN CASE OF AN EMERGENCY

Once again just as a holiday approaches, this time, Thanksgiving, I was dumped at the vet to remain caged up for a week as the Bonzos trot off to places afar and asunder, this time Hawaii. "They have been there before to Maui but not to the Big Island which is their destination this time. By all accounts a place in appearance that resembles the moon, but with tarmac and traffic signals.

While they wallow in mahi mahi and seared ahi, seeing how many weak jokes they can muster about all the lava on the island, paraphrasing songs for example such as 'Lava come back to me' and 'Dream Lava' I'm left to contemplate what could have been, on a Thanksgiving at home, scraps of turkey perhaps or a double helping of treats. This year all I have with me is a couple of toys, of which I am fond, and get walkies twice a day.

The Bonzos splashed out for this trip, opting to stay at the ritzy Four Seasons a vast resort spread over a wide area, with it's tropical paradise setting, miles of pathway between rooms and bungalows lush sandy beaches enticing pools and a spa, a place Mrs. Bonzo can't resist.

It was as I understand it, after one of her jaunts for a massage, that Mr. Bonzo thought he should familiarize himself with the Safety Information provided to all guests as prescribed in the Hotel Directory, he had little else to do, every time she goes for one of these adventures, she returns mesmerized, groggy and in no condition for activity, other than a quiet nap.

Mr. Bonzo often appears this way, without the aid of spa treatments.

As she was nodding off, Mr. Bonzo insisted she listen to safety procedures according to the Gospel of the Four Seasons, and he quoted verbatim.

Mr. Bonzo "It says here, in the event of a fire emergency, become familiar with the walkways, how are we going to do that, we can't even find our way back to the room.

It also says, study the layout of your room. Well the bed is in the middle, and we have two chairs, so when it says here 'Inspect anything that might help or hinder possible escape' what's to inspect. "Note the location of your fire extinguisher" he informed his beloved, well the extinguisher is in the closet in case of fire, behind your seven suitcases, twenty two outfits you brought with, and my thong, for which, by the way, I shall be eternally grateful to you for allowing me to pack, in one of your many suitcases, I like traveling light, having become accustomed to it.

Mrs. Bonzo remained motionless, and considered herself immune to conversation, as is usually the case if a thong is mentioned.

"It also says, and I quote "Always keep your room key card handy near your bed.' What good is that if the room burns down, since every time we get one of these hotel room cards, they rarely work, and we have to go back to the reception for another one, besides if, because of fire, there is no room left, we can just advance into the space, the one with the burnt bed and two burnt chairs ! he spluttered, and not knowing when to stop, adding "A space previously occupied by your many suitcases."

Still motionless Mrs. Bonzo declined to comment, but connoisseurs of a situation like this, where a napping massaged wife was under harassment, might understand, that Mrs. Bonzo raised one eyebrow, and that said it all.

"Listen to this" he continued, "Persons discovering a fire should remain calm, and go to the nearest fire pull station, I haven't seen one of those have you?" Still no response, from the napping Mrs. Bonzo, but he blindly soldiered on with "After you have pulled the alarm, tell the operator the exact nature of the trouble, smoke, fire, heat, sparks etc., well there has not been to many sparks in our bedroom" he said in a low voice. "It goes on to say, state exactly where the trouble is and how serious," Mr Bonzo reflected for a minute and thought the answer to that must be the thong.

He went on "To evacuate your room take your room key card, why in the world would we take that, if the room burns down? "Still no response from the dozing Mrs. Bonzo. "Then it says, keep a wet cloth over nose and mouth, and proceed to the main lobby, he added however, where no doubt you will find hundreds of guest with wet towels over their noses, waving their room card, shouting I couldn't find the fire pull station either.

There followed a few minutes silence, as Mr. Bonzo was reading items that at last appeared to make sense, but this brief moment was shattered by an out burst of giggling, followed by belly laughs and the occasional guffaw.

"Ocean and beach safety, dear, it says here, never turn your back on the ocean. How would you return to shore, walk backwards? It also says, avoid the ocean if you are not in good physical condition, that applies to almost every guest here, no wonder the beaches are empty.

Still not amused, Mrs. Bonzo sank into oblivion, as the land of nod seemed a much more attractive proposition, than the incessant Mr. Bonzo.

"Can you believe this" continued Mr. Bonzo, "It actually says, never swim or dive in unexplored water, where are we, up the Amazon, near the source of the Blue Nile? It goes on to say, waves come in sets, small and large, and patterns are inconsistent." Rather like my underwear from KMart he bemused. "Then there's the warning flags, red indicates dangerous conditions, red and yellow hazardous conditions, yellow, medium wind. I should put out a yellow flag out every morning before I go into the bathroom" he thought to himself.

"Now hear this," Mr. Bonzo shouted as if an announcer at an army barracks, actually he said it twice. "Coral Polyps are found in shallow waters and have poisonous tentacles and any contact should be treated immediately with alcohol or household vinegar, then wash the wound with baking soda and water. How are we going to find all of that, walking backwards to the shore, surely there isn't a market in unexplored waters, maybe there is an amazon.com" once again he chuckled to himself, seemingly having a good time all on his own.

Mrs. Bonzo had not stirred from her nap, but awoke on hearing the shrill voice of her husband, "In these cases call from the fire pull station." What fire pull station" she murmured, the one by the golf course?"

Displaying utter shock Mr. Bonzo with mouth agape and obviously startled, responded with "You know where it is" "Of course" she replied, "We passed it yesterday, when you got lost, returning from breakfast, don't you remember, you knew of a short cut, to our room, and by the time we found it under your exquisite leadership it was time for lunch. Actually we passed it four times, as we got lost on the way to breakfast."

At this point, having had fantasies of being the hero, in case of an emergency, and somewhat disgusted that the massaged Mrs. Bonzo knew of the existence of a fire pull station, and of course he didn't, Mr. Bonzo declined to read on. Instead he opted for a walk on the beach, blue waters awash with surf, the trade winds blowing, swaying palm trees and in the distance puffy clouds on the horizon. He lazily set on his jaunt, with a wet towel around his nose, and of course clutching his room key card. Behind him Mrs. Bonzo was waving frantically and in earnest shouting "Do you know you are not wearing any shorts"

Now that's an emergency.

Chapter 25

THE MAINE ATTRACTION

As I lay on the kitchen floor quietly, listening to the Bonzos organizing yet another trip, I felt consumed in the idea yet again I would be boarded at the vet, while they gallivant to places unknown to me, and that I will probably never see, or experience.

With both of them sitting around the kitchen table preparing to book flights and hotels, I couldn't help wondering about which destination has now taken their fancy, I am rarely informed. Perhaps there are off to some exotic far away tropical paradise, even a remote island of the coast of somewhere, or the most likely... a retirement home, although I can't see Mrs. Bonzo amongst the elderly, she always looks so young and vivacious, Mr. Bonzo on the other hand might be a perfect fit.

I caught snippets of information about a remote town in Northern Maine near the Canadian border, not off the coast of anywhere, and hardly tropical, since they would take heavy clothing due to inclement weather and were likely to freeze their buns off. Not like them I thought, doesn't sound as if they would be sipping drinks through a straw or sunbathing, maybe the retirement home isn't too far off base.

As their discussion went back and forth on the merits of which winter woolies Mr. Bonzo must take since there was an expectation he could discover frostbite on arrival, I am left to consider my fate once again in the small confines of Stickem In a Cage Boarding, not much to look forward to.

The day came when I witnessed the bag being packed that always accompanies me to the vet, stuffed with toys and a few treats, and a special goodbye hug before being loaded into the car.

The Bonzos on the other hand were full of anticipation, off to the airport to Boston and then a commuter plane to Presque Isle, wherever that may be, pick up a rental car and drive north. I'm sure they will try to tell me on their return, but as far as I was concerned it was hardly a "Main Event", it wasn't until they returned that my senses were numbed.

"Zak, we are all going to live in Maine" he said the day I was rescued from Hotel Boarding, "We have bought a house, on five acres" he persisted, "With trees and a pond, what do you think of that." I had just returned home familiarizing myself with my usual home- stead surroundings, as this bombshell hit, talk about total insecurity, and they wonder why I keep chewing my paws. People chew finger nails, I chew paws. Every living thing finds solace somehow.

"You are going to love it" he persisted, as my early puppy hood facial expression of stark blank amazement began to form, and clearly showing bewilderment. Mrs. Bonzo approached me with her usual loving care but also waded in with how wonderful life will be in the rural surroundings of a small town in Northern Maine, living on five acres, "You will be able to run and scamper at will" she said, just adding to what was already a shock to my system.

All I have known is life in the land of sunglasses, beach umbrellas and freeway traffic, walks on a leash, an occasional romp in the park, smog and lazy hazy days of summer, affording me the luxury of countless naps as and when I felt like it, and the run of the garden over which I considered myself 'Lord of the Manor' Now it seems I am to be thrust into four seasons, some of it very cold according to the Bonzos, but the big news is, I can run and scamper at will!

"Zak where we are going, will be a big change" Mr. Bonzo explained, "It's peaceful, serene, and we are going to enjoy ourselves now we are retired."

It had occurred to me I had been seeing a lot of the Bonzos lately, they were home every day, not leaving me on my own, and we seemed to do a lot more together, is that what retired means. I had heard them talking about retirement recently, but took little notice since I couldn't imagine how that would affect me.

"Our new house is a hundred years old" Mr. Bonzo profoundly stated, so it seems are you, I thought, maybe this move is into a retirement home, what would become of me. It was while pondering life and its meaning once again, as I was stretched out with my paws widespread, dealing with early stages of another depression' that Mrs. Bonzo weighed in with another of her 'Incomings will also have a barn" she blurted out. Now you must realize I had no idea what a barn was, for all I knew it could be something that goes in the kitchen. This was followed various joyous statements of what we will have, and yet I was not impressed, how could I be, with no picture in my head as to how life would be with all these benefits the Bonzos seem to feel will enhance life for the three of us.

What are they thinking at their time of life, and all they spoke to about their new rural life in the country seemed to generate the same response, are they going senile? It's a question I have asked myself for some time now, in fact since I arrived at the Bonzo domain. I tried to relax but just couldn't help chewing my paws again.

In the middle of my thoughts yet another 'Incoming' shot forth from Mrs. Bonzo, "I still can't get over the Mrs. Moose we saw" she giggled to Mr. Bonzo, "There were two of them" he replied, both ugly and a chocolate color, that's where chocolate mousse comes from" he spluttered, "Wonder what the plural ofmoose is" he said with a grin, "Mooses or probably Moosei." he added, followed by multiple puns such as if they played the piano they would be Moosicians and so on.

He rambled on with other possibilities, and then proceeded to advise me the moose is the official state animal of Maine. When you think about it, that's silly, all the best restaurants in the USA are proud and happy to offer Maine lobster, when available, and patrons clamor for the chance of it, in towns and cities across America, it's a big attraction on the menu, shouldn't the state symbol of Maine be a lobster?

It seems by the roadside in Northern Maine there are numerous signs showing the possibility that a moose may appear, this sign depicts a picture of a male moose, naturally with antlers, I wonder if there is a National Organization of Women Moose who can protest that they are not represented.

One night while watching TV, a commercial appeared demonstrating a rotating contraption that spread lime grass seed over lawns that obviously needed it, Mrs Bonzo could not hold back her thoughts of Mr. Bonzo sitting on a drive mower for the first time in his life, playing the role of gentleman farmer, in Northern Maine's inclement weather, dressed in farming attire but hopefully not wearing jodhpurs. That is not something I would hope to witness.

"You'll need one of those" she stated emphatically.

"One of what" replied the soon to be bumbling farmer. "A whirly thing" she responded.

I could for once see it coming, Mr. Bonzo taking a trip to the local hardware store, and sauntering up to the clerk at the counter, in perfectly groomed jodhpurs, a hat with ear muffs, and boots, Mr Bonzo that is, not the clerk.

Mr. Bonzo "Do you have a whirly thing."

Clerk "I beg your pardon."

Mr. Bonzo "A whirly thing to spread seed."

Clerk "Come again."

Mr. Bonzo "A whirly thing to spread your seed."

Clerk "Whether I have a whirly one or not, is no concern of yours.

Mr. Bonzo "How do you spread your seeds then."

Clerk "Look here Mister, we don't tolerate that kind of language or inquisition here in Maine, we view these kind of topics as extremely personal."

Mr. Bonzo: I don't think you understand, my wife says I need a whirly thing.

Clerk: I'm sure you do, and please offer my sympathies on her predicament, but don't expect me to help out.

This scenario probably ending in Mr. Bonzo being banned from the store for life, and gaining a bad reputation all over town, all because Mrs. Bonzo was trying to be helpful. Knowing Mr. Bonzo he would immediately go to another store, hoping word had not yet spread in the retail world.

Also knowing him, he would think of something else needed'
such as an espresso machine, something he has not has much luck
with in the past, according to him because of thin steamers. Since
there is no Starbucks for at least one hundred miles, and neither
of them could manage without their lattes and cappuccinos,
the purchase of an espresso machine would eventually become
mandatory, and on a personal note, that means one trip a day I
won't get to go on.

I could visualize him however stumble upon another hardware
store, this one displaying household items familiar to the local
inhabitants, and in concert with the County surroundings, probably
named General Store, no doubt after a victorious army general in
days of yore.

Once again he would saunter up to a counter, only this time a
female clerk would be in attendance.

Mr. Bonzo: Do you have a wide steamer?

Female Clerk: Ugh!

Mr. Bonzo: One that blows fairly well.

Female Clerk: Were you in the other hardware store a few
minutes ago?

Mr. Bonzo: Goodbye.

In the ensuing days after the grand announcement the Bonzos
decided to give their new house a name, but as usual with much
banter between them could not agree. Each time Mr. Bonzo sug
gested something, the reply back to him was that, it sounds like a
boat or a horse.

Mrs. Bonzo stated "It should sound like a proper name" to
which his response was "How about Rosie?"

The scornful look on her face needed no explanation, she was
not amused.

Eventually Mrs. Bonzo came up with something, they could
both live with... Havenhill, one wonders how long that will last
how much of a haven will it be in the depths of winter, will I hav
to learn to ski, or skate on thin ice on the frozen pond, will they
get me a wooly coat, I just hate those things, will my water freeze,
I can't imagine what my whirly will feel like.

IF ONLY I COULD TELL THEM

As usual I wandered to my humble but favorite place in front of the fireplace, and considered we are likely to embark on a disaster, probably as three blind moose, we'll see how well, we run and scamper at will.

Chapter 26

THE SOFT SHOE SHUFFLE

Since the Bonzos are retired and I see so much more of them, I see things about them perhaps I didn't notice before. They are getting older, more forgetful, although in Mr. Bonzo's case due to obvious mental impairment, that would not be difficult, I think also they have completely lost their marbles, going soft in the head. They put the house up for sale, how absurd is that, my whole life has been wrapped up in this abode, now they are selling it?

After consultation with real estate agents, a notice went up on the front lawn, something I witnessed as we were about to embark on a neighborhood jaunt. Sadly it was placed exactly where I like to pee before our daily stroll. Of course I can't read, and I'm sure it had the usual real estate language, but in my mind it probably should have stated;

FOR SALE
ZAKS' HOUSE
BEAUTIFULLY APPOINTED, MODEL HOME OFFERED BY TWO SENILE LUNATICS MOVING TO MAINE WOULD SUIT SINGLE WHEATEN TERRIER

Ever since the notice went up, and agents everywhere seemed to get wind of it, there was a constant stream of people, ringing the door bell. As soon as the melodic chimes went off, I was immediately expected to dash into the garden out of harms way, as curious prospective buyers enter. After the first couple of times, I decided to stand my ground, or at the very least be elusive, after all this is, *my* house and the doorbell drives me crazy, it sounds like the Pizza commercial on TV.

I had to sit outside the sliding doors, seemingly forever and peer into the house, to observe this ritual of 'Viewing the Home.' I was expected to be quiet, well behaved and just be on the sidelines while strangers intrude. Have you ever watched people view houses, their first instinct is to glance up at the ceiling. Now I ask you, how many people intend to reside up there. their eyes roam all over the first room they enter, and they continue to concentrate on walls and ceilings, by the time they have seen the last room there is a distinct let's get out of here look about them.

They also shuffle along, nobody strides at a brisk pace, and when couples view together, it seems only the ladies show any interest, it reminds me of disenchanted husbands at a mall, tagging along because their wives insist, as they preferred to do something else.

Whoever these prospective buyers are, they are always accompanied by their own real estate agent, often pointing to what they think are the good points of the house, and yet none of the agents have seen it before. How do they know the good points. It also seems to me nobody asks intelligent questions, they are always relating to financial matters, nobody asks questions like "Is the roof likely to fall off' or 'Is there a good reason why there are only little patches of grass left on what appears to have been the lawn', I always considered myself a great pisser!

Everyone seems to notice me sitting quietly, nose pressed up against the glass door, and as might be expected, visitors constantly ask "What kind of dog is that" to which if I had my way, would have answered, "One that wants to stay here."

I must say though, I did get a lot of compliments, but it seems only from dog owners, those that are not, are wary of me, they probably imagine I am going to thrust myself upon them, like a missile about to launch, I have been tempted. Dog lovers pet me, and make a fuss of me, don't they know I prefer the Bonzos to do that, however it makes me feel good, and gives my ego a boost.

One time an agent came with the buyers, and I took an instant dislike to her, she strutted around the place, without much to say, looking as if she owned the place, and didn't seem to offer any good points. You know how humans can take an instant dislike to other people, so can Wheatons, when she stepped into the garden, I peed on her shoes. Mr. Bonzo had to get the garden hose out to douse her down, that made me feel even better.

She shot off at a brisk pace through the garden gate and informed everybody she would wait outside, it seemed to me I had found the ideal way to stop the shuffle. I am fairly sure she was not a dog lover, and if not, after this event, less of one.

You may be curious as to what the Bonzos do when these visitors are coming. Before their arrival they are frantically cleaning up. This has become a daily affair, something Mrs. Bonzo has not had to do in years, and clearly has no plans to continue the practice. However she has not lost her will to delegate much of it, Mr. Bonzo being the recipient of her instructions. He is getting quite proficient with a vacuum cleaner, I know that because it's the only thing Mrs. Bonzo doesn't complain about after his efforts at housekeeping are completed. In everything else he got an 'F'.

Grade, this was noticeable because he kept muttering to himself constantly, each phrase seemingly beginning with an F.

During shuffle time, they stand by quietly, waiting for silly questions, or to see if there is any real interest, it's almost like hospital patients when visitors arrive and no one quite knows what to say. When asked where are they moving to, and prospects discover the locale, there is a distinct perplexed look from possible buyers, as if to say "Do you know how very cold it is in winter in Maine?" or "Why on earth would you want to leave Southern California?" and the ultimate put down for me "Will your dog have a wooly coat?" It was during one of these inquisitions I overhead Mrs. Bonzo talk about a small town called Fort Kent, it was the first time I knew where the new house was located, and it may be no coincidence that also begins with an F.

The Bonzos can be quite charming, Mrs. Bonzo clearly the leader in the charm department, patient and very soft in her demeanor to others, she plainly was leading the 'Soft Shoe Shuffle.'

Chapter 27

REFLECTIONS

It seems we really are moving, the realtor brought the good tidings to the Bonzos that the house was sold. I didn't know If I should laugh or cry, they really are going to a new house, without consulting me as usual, they didn't know If I could make the transition or not. were consumed with forms to fill out provided by their smiling realtor, boy did I know who to pee on next.

Everyone was so happy you would have thought they sold the leaning tower of Pisa, now that's a local listing!

Some of these forms were a talking point between husband and wife, that I couldn't be a party to yet, had no choice but to listen to them asking each other how to answer simple questions. One question under disclosures it appears, asks 'In the last three years has anyone died on the property.' I couldn't help thinking the answer must be yes, I remember Mrs. Bonzo telling her spouse she thought he had some nights when sleeping in his leather bound armchair.

On another form, questions are asked about numerous items that may or may not be listed to be included in the property, such as a sauna, hot tub and sprinklers. How I wished they had a hot tub, the only delight I have had in getting soaked is my sprinkler run. Another relates to a quick release mechanism on bedroom windows, there have been many times I thought it would have been nice to have one of those in the cages at the vet, when boarding.

Mr. Bonzo giggled when reading aloud the following question, 'Is the property located within one mile of a former federal or state ordnance location, such as a military training center.' Without any intro, rather like one of Mrs. Bonzo's incomings, he said to her "I wonder if they mean that sign we saw once a few miles down the road, Army Reserve Center, which I thought meant if the first choice Center could not be used, try the Reserve Center!" As is the custom with her, there was little response from Mrs. Bonzo.

He misread one question, he thought it said 'Is the property a condom or planned development' "Hey, he said to her, that's getting a bit personal isn't it?" Mrs. Bonzo straightened him out "I think it reads condominium.

The buyers arranged to have the house inspected, and I shuddered to think of all the things that may have been wrong with it, they probably didn't notice, such as, no dog run, and no access to the outside world for Wheatons, but as events turned out, it passed muster, luckily Mr. Bonzo didn't have to be inspected.

The days after the sold notice went up, the Bonzos were busy with preparations for the big move, life went on as usual for me. Most days were spent calling movers trying to make travel arrangements and generally make the whole thing a well planned operation. I have been with the Bonzos long enough to know, not much turns out to be a well planned operation.

The first call Mr. Bonzo made to movers, went something like this...

Mr. Bonzo: "Hello is this Movem and Shakem, we would like a quote for moving to Maine."

Moving Person: "Are you nuts, what do want to move there for. Don't you know how cold it is in the winter?

Mr. Bonzo: "Funny you should say that, a lot of people have told us that."

Moving Person: "We don't move too many people there."

Mr. Bonzo: "Why not?"

Moving Person: "'Because we don't go to Maine," and he added "Unless we take a wrong turn on the way to somewhere else."

I took little notice, until I kept hearing my name mentioned when they called airlines. They were making arrangements to ship me to the East Coast, and It was not something I was looking forward to, if I was going to fly, the least they could do was get me a window seat in first class. All I could decipher out of their

110

conversations was the size of the cage needed in which I was to be transported.

I had flashbacks to the time I left Iowa by truck as a young innocent puppy, not knowing what my future prospects would be, here I am again not knowing what lies ahead, isn't it strange how life can seem to go full circle.

This was the time I gave thought to writing my memoirs, I didn't know if I could remember much about life in California once I arrived in Maine. While the Bonzos were rearranging their lives and mine, I thought this the best time gather my thoughts.

I can't say it has been too eventful, but what would I have done without the Bonzos? What would my life have been like, would I have been better off, I don't think so. I have all the love from them any intelligent fun loving Wheaten could want, and I love them so much warts and all.

They let me share everything with them, I like being involved. I have had a comfortable life, and now an adventure to which if truth be told, I can look forward. I am about to become a country animal, new pastures to explore and who knows new memories to forge, and perhaps some time in the future I can add more to my reflections.

Chapter 28

MOVE THEM AND SHAKE ME

The dreaded day arrived, after two weeks of packing up, stumbling over boxes, numerous trips to the packing store, mostly for scotch tape, which Mr. Bonzo was always losing or more often, the subject of his scathing comments when the strips came off the roll and he couldn't get a full dose of the tape to use. I noticed several rolls being tossed into the trash accompanied by foul language just as Mrs. Bonzo asked for a roll. A lot of it stuck to his fingers, and other parts of his anatomy and was still there by the time he retired for the night.

Naturally there was those crucial decisions by Mrs. Bonzo as to what was going with us, and what was not, Mr. Bonzo is absolved of such responsibility. It seems before they were married, they decided all the day to day domestic decisions Mrs. Bonzo would make, all the major decisions would be Mr. Bonzo's...in decades there have been no major decisions to be made, luckily for him.

The movers were to arrive early, and load the neatly stacked boxes stored in the garage, and then cart them off to Maine. I was carted off to be bathed at the nearby grooming place. Just when there is a lot of different activity, they want me out of the way, Don't they know I could have helped.

It seems movers were more than unimpressed that altogether they had to load some two hundred boxes, Mr. Bonzo felt some satisfaction that it took only 99 rolls of scotch tape in the process of packing.

The foreman of the crew suggested to Mrs. Bonzo that that was a lot of boxes for two people, "Two and a Wheaton Terrier" she replied. "How many boxes does the dog have? He inquired, "None" she replied.

Some hours after they waved farewell to the belongings, seeing a lifetime of accumulation stacked in one small part of a very large truck , hoping the driver knew where the new house is located, in the remote part of nowhere, I was rescued from the bathing heaven. I quite like a bath , love the bubbles, it spruces me up, gives me a feeling of well being, and smell nice, but did they have to do this to me on moving day.

To my surprise I was returned to base in a strange car, one they had rented, since their cars were conveyed on transporter hopefully to arrive in one piece, or since there were two of them, in two pieces.

On arrival at home it should have been no surprise that there was no furniture in what was completely empty house. I was taken aback, and searched every room for something familiar, how strange I felt, How life sometimes goes round and round to the beginning again, on my arrival at the Bonzo's many moons ago, I did the same thing, went from room to room to investigate, how empty it all now feels.

There was still one last piece of packing, suitcases for the Bonzo's attire, for the trip and the time they would have to wait for the moving truck to arrive in Maine, some ten days or so. Somehow they can never seem to get this sort of thing right, too many clothes, too little room in the cases, and too few of those. I had no such problem a few of my favorite toys in a paper bag was to accompany me, and they were packed and ready to fly, I however wasn't. After sitting on suitcases one after the other, hoping all their stuff would cram in, and Mr. Bonzo falling off them continuously, I took great pride in knowing I was packed.

During one of Mr. Bonzo's falling episodes, the doorbell rang and in came the realtors who sold the house, with gifts for the Bonzos, two overlarge bathroom robes with their names on it. I thought pensively for a moment and considered they must have got the names wrong, it should have been Mr. and Mrs. Senile on the small breast pocket. I wondered why I didn't get one, after all Zak is only three letters and at my size I could have proudly stuffed one in my paperbag.

Although very much appreciated, the only case that they managed to close had to be reopened, to accommodate their new attire. I left the house for a last look at the garden I was not going to be a witness to a repeat of case stuffing.

Dear garden, I mused I wonder how many times I have peed on you, strolled through the bushes, and ruined what was, when I arrived a thriving lawn, and flower haven, such fond memories.

Some time later with a number of suitcases, most of them with shirt sleeves, jeans and two robes hanging out of the sides, we bade a fond farewell to the house waved to neighbors, and set off for the airport, with a rather large looking cage on the back seat next to me, housing my paper bag with toys in it, nothing hanging out though.

Naturally before reaching the airport, they had to stop at a Starbucks for the last time, taking in their favorite beverages, and ordering water for me. I lapped it up, I was thirsty, but unaware they slipped me a Mickey Finn, in the form of a sleeping pill provided by the vet. It took no time at all for me to feel drowsy, tired, listless and woozy, like Mr. Bonzo on one of his good days.

I wasn't asleep when I was herded into the cage on arrival at the airport, but I knew it wasn't going to be too long before snooze time would come. The line for check in was so long Mr. Bonzo joined the end of it somewhere in the distance, so far that perhaps he was at another airport, while I curled up in my cage chaperoned by Mrs. Bonzo near the counter awaiting the eventual arrival of her husband to the front of the line, by the time he arrived I think I was in the land of nod, but not quite out of it, at least awake enough to feel the shaking from being transported on a trolley for boarding.

It was a night flight to Boston, and at Mrs. Bonzo's suggestion her spouse digested a sleeping pill of his own just before boarding. He always has trouble sleeping on aircraft, so I thought he should travel in his favorite armchair, he has no trouble sleeping in that.

It seems he fell asleep while walking down the aisle to his seat, Mrs. Bonzo propped him up, until she could push him into a sitting position, she had great difficulty and the two of them waltzed toward their seats locked together. From other passengers

point of view who were already seated, it looked as though they might be trying to accomplish mile high club" status, despite the aircraft still attached to the jetway. A lot of muttering could be heard from Row 5 to the rear. I on the other hand was fast asleep below the main cabin as cargo, with no seat, no lighting, no toilet facilities, and definitely no in flight meal service, however this was compensated by a considerable dose of turbulence from time to time, enough to rattle my cage and shake me.

As dawn approached and the aircraft was ready to land Mr. Bonzo aroused from his slumber, to the wails of the flight attendant, familiar to frequent flyers with instructions concerning the fastening of seat belts and returning the flight attendant to the upright position, continuing with instructions on reaching the terminal. Mrs. Bonzo was already spruced and ready for deplaning, as the attendant wailed on, Mr. Bonzo remarked to her, how he too hates the reference to the word 'Terminal' when flying.

This was naturally followed by another announcement, this time from the pilot, who sensibly declared "thanks for flying with Herdem Like Sheep Airways, we know you have a choice of bankrupt airlines, so thanks for choosing us."

Fortunately on this occasion there was no repeat of a previous flight they took returning to Southern California's main airport, when the rather flushed announcer proclaimed "We would like to welcome you to Los Angeles, however the pilot made a booboo and we are in San Diego."

They had no problem identifying their luggage at baggage claim, for obvious shirt sleeve and robe reasons, and proceeded to a special baggage section to await my arrival, shaking cage and all. I stirred slowly after a trolley on which my cage was perched came to an abrupt stop. I felt warmed to see the Bonzos who greeted me with much glee, as if I had flown solo for the first time, well almost.

So the first leg of the journey was complete without incident, and we were on the East Coast, in the midst of scurrying passengers' taxis, buses and tall gray buildings, didn't look much like remote countryside living at all. Mr. Bonzo left us to pick up a rental can and when he returned I was lifted on to the back seat, still a little drowsy ready for the long drive north. Some hours later, Mr. Bonzo out how to get out of the airport having circled numerous times, and we hit the interstate.

After driving all day, we neared our destination, as my apprehension grew, Mr. Bonzo remarked how he had never seen so many barns in his life, as farmland scenery swept by, and the smell of potatoes filled the air. I had never seen anything like it, where were the tall palm trees, hoards of freeway traffic, police chases, road rage, blue skies and sandy beaches ?

Slowly I was coming round from an apparent drug overdose, to be my normal self again just in time to hear the Bonzos proclaim, "We're here" as they entered the long driveway leading up to a gray and white house with a long porch surrounded by lots of green grass, actually most of it turned out to be weeds I found out later, and a barn. Well I contemplated, as I looked at the Bonzos, here's another barn for your viewing pleasure.

As we stretched our legs and took in the country air, I sniffed my way around the outside of the house setting my sights on good peeing territory, it seemed to me there were acres of it. I did however notice a strange odor, and was taken by surprise to see large animals in the distance standing motionless. Mr. Bonzo seeing me stare at them, whispered "Those are cows, Zak." I was still staring at them when one of them mooed, I was so shaken at the sound, I jumped back three paces in disbelief and made for the front door of the house for safe haven.

I entered and unleashed, went from room to room on another investigative trail. It was larger than our previous house and had wooden floors ideal for a wheaten to skate on.

There were packages awaiting our arrival, since the Bonzos had the forethought to ship utensils in advance, knowing their stuff wouldn't arrive for a while, I could help noticing one package had a saucepan handle sticking out of the side of it, true to form I thought.

As the Bonzos went from room to room, making sure all was in order, they disappeared up a staircase. I am not going up one of those things I said to myself, and to this day I never have. After all the Bonzos never showed me how to climb stairs, probably because we didn't have them in the house in Sunny California.

ZAK

I was more inclined to take another look outside, there was so much space, so many trees, wildlife flying, and a herd of smelly cows still motionless. I barked at them, but they just stood there ignoring me, probably thought I was a City Slicker. Some animals have the ability to send messages to others, had it been a moose I could have sent something in moose code. I tried in barking format "I'm Zak, just arrived, we are going to live here in the country, without a robe with my name on it." Nothing however seemed to move them, or shake them.

It was a long journey and I was tired, too tired to stand and chatter idly with motionless cattle, there would be another day where I could survey the new homestead at my leisure, take in all the sights and sounds that rural Maine had to offer. I could run among the trees, muddy my paws, dive into the pond that sits at the foot of the hillside and scare the ducks, discover bird watching, so much to look forward to, maybe I would like it here after all. I laid down on the floor so tired nothing would move me or shake me.

Chapter 29

ONE MAINE STREET FOR THE DEAR HUNTERS

The next morning as the Bonzos descended the staircase, from their bedroom upstairs, I greeted them warmly, I had spent the night alone for the first time in my life. In California I slept in their bedroom, next to their bed, but since I decided not to climb the staircase in this house, I was on my own and it was like camping out, as there was no furniture around.

"We're going in to town Zak" advised Mr. Bonzo, "We have to pick up groceries." he went on, it will be your first chance to see Fort Kent. Mrs. Bonzo had made a list of items needed, and when she does this, they usually quickly, run out of scrap paper. Elhis time being the initial grocery run, Mr. Bonzo suggested they organize it into volumes like history books, volume one... produce, volume two ...canned stuff, volume three ...hair spray for Mrs. Bonzo and so On. I knew I would be put on the back seat of the car left alone while they entered a store, but it was an opportunity to scout the terrain. Where is town and how far is it?

We set off, and with much expectation I sat on the back seat, my eyes fixed through the window, at the countryside still wondering what the big attraction was for the Bonzos. Near our house we passed a farm, sonr potato fields, more farms and some twenty minutes later we sccmed to come across civilization as a small town came into view, I first saw a (no longer used train station', and according to Mr. Bonzo it was an historic building, it didn't look historic to me, not that I would know what anything historic would look like. Further on, a left turn into the one main street opened the way for Mr. Bonzo to give me his tourist guide speech.

"Look Zak, this little town is very compact, see, on the right, there is the church, next to it the funeral parlor, a real estate agent and an insurance agency, all within fifty yards. Ihat means you can die, have the service, be buried, sell the house and collect on the insurance, all at one time." Taking a leaf out of Mrs. Bonzo's book, I was not amused.

The town really had only one main street, which rumor has it doubles up as the airport runway, it had charm, probably hadn't changed in fifty years, I don't think the Bonzos had, so maybe the attraction was to became clear to me. Sitting in the parking lot of the market, I noticed there were a lot of trucks around, new ones, old ones, big ones, small ones but no Mercedes, BMW's or convertibles, California must haves.

The Bonzos returned with numerous shopping carts and little room left in the car for me.

Mr. Bonzo continued his guided tour pointing out various landmarks including what was called the 'International Bridge.' spans the St. Johns river and leads to Canada, foreign soil to me.

"Why is it called the International Bridge" inquired Mrs. Bonzo.

"Probably because a foreigner crossed it once" retorted Mr. Bonzo.

"See on the left here, there's even a Chinese restaurant" he added, maybe a Chinaman crossed the bridge I thought.

I was not seeing any pet shops, where they have doggie treats, I contemplated. Just as I was thinking about that, we stopped in a gas station, in the middle of town.

"Fill her up" said Mr. Bonzo to the attendant, as he rolled the window down. "What a cute dog" the attendant remarked looking at me as if he had no idea what breed I was, welcome to the rest of the world I thought.

"Can he have a treat" he went on. "Sure" responded the Bonzos, and a few moments later he returned with a doggie biscuit. I love treats, always have, so I snatched it out of his hand, and it didn't take long for me to believe this indeed was a wonderful little town. How often do we fill up with gas I wondered, can we come back tomorrow ? The tour continued on the way home, and now my interest was peaked, arc there any other places they give out treats or do you have to go hunting for them. I snuggled up to my towel on the back seat with a view of providing myself with a guided tour of my new pastures when I got home.

The Bonzos on their return started a clean up campaign, in preparation for the big day when all their belongings would arrive, if the moving van would ever find us. I was left to set off on safari around the estate.

By comparison to 'home' in California, this house certainly was different. It was surrounded by acres of grass, birch trees everywhere, a nice view of a pond and good hunting ground for a wheaten. I scampered toward the pond, full of the joys of spring, well actually, it was late summer, passing raspberry bushes, muddy patches, with the aroma of motionless cattle around me, in search of wildlife. The thought occurred to me however, what if I found some, what would I do? I'd never been hunting, for that matter I don't recall any Bonzo memories of them on safari.

I sat down facing the pond, and considered, that if the Bonzos ever went hunting, Mr. Bonzo with a rifle over his shoulder, would probably be a severe danger to mankind, animals on the other hand would have no problem, while Mrs. Bonzo would be dressed for the occasion, sporting a fur hat, fur coat, looking like a Polish singer in a Klezmer band.

It was during my quiet time in the fields of play, I realized how different this all was, the open space, the country air, flies everywhere. I scampered through the birch trees, around the barn, back toward the house feeling pretty good about myself, when a booming voice bellowed "Zak, where are you?" It was Mr. Bonzo in search of me, not a deer or a moose, and he was waving a broomstick in the air, not a rifle. This gave me the idea that I could disappear behind the trees and have him look for me, hopefully unsuccessfully. I decided to keep that under my hat for a future time.

The clean up was still going on as I entered the house, muddy paws and all, when I encountered a stern looking Mrs. Bonzo. "Zak, I've just cleaned the kitchen floor, don't corne in here with muddy paws" she barked. kitchen floor has to be clean, I can't keep on wiping up the mud you bring in" she continued. This pattern of bringing in the mud would however, continue and even to this day, she complains, however I am pleased to report the culprit is no longer me, Mr. Bonzo earned his own distinction.

As they sprayed, mopped and wiped, I lay down on the newly cleaned kitchen floor listening to each of them bellowing from different parts of the house to each other, 'Come and look at this or that.' Most often because this house has many more rooms and is so much bigger, and they constantly went hunting for each other, I heard a lot of.. .'Dear where are you?

I simply lay there mulling over the fact that the town had one main treat.

Chapter 30

THE LONELY ROAD

The next event was to be the arrival of the moving van, some ten days after leaving California, and a considerable dose of unpacking. For the Bonzos it seemed an eternity, it didn't make any difference to me, but they were also waiting for their cars to arrive, and after several attempts to find their whereabouts there seemed to me some dismay on their part, that it would take forever for anything to arrive.

I on the other hand continued my exploration of wooded areas and became extremely proficient at collecting burrs, prickly stuff, leaves and an assorted array of old dry horticulture upon my fur.

Then a phone call, sheer delight upon the faces of the Bonzos, the truck with 'Their stuff was arriving the next day. From the kitchen window you can see the road that most traffic use to get in and out of town. Mrs. Bonzo calls it the lonely road, since there is hardly any traffic, and you can't tell where it's going. I would like to know where it goes, hopefully California, should I ever want to go back there.

In the distance they could see the van, and for once they knew where it was going... in our driveway. Boxes upon boxes were dumped in the house, each marked with where they were going to be set down, unfortunately all markings on the box as to which room they were to be placed didn't seem to affect the unloading crew, so most were dumped in the living room for the Bonzos to sort out.

It was good to see familiar furniture, and things I had become accustomed to having around me, it started to feel like home. After an all day event of unloading, the truck and crew departed, and so started the chaos of putting everything away, where Mrs. Bonzo wanted. All I cared about was where my treats were going to be stored, so I could sit by the cupboard when the need for a snack arose.

It was during their unpacking mode, and a need for me to pee, that I wandered outside and looked at the lonely road, something worth an investigation. I started a little jaunt south, I could faintly hear the Bonzos in the background shouting something about me returning to base, when several cars seemed to be heading in my direction, from the north as well as the south, I turned my head and saw Mr. Bonzo waving frantically. He was huffing and puffing and seemed awfully red in the face, all traffic stopped, many with screeching brakes. What's all the fuss about I thought, as Mr. Bonzo caught up with me, only because I sat down in the road, hoping to get a ride.

One of the drivers poked her head out of the window and asked What kind of dog is that?" Mr. Bonzo was short in his response, "Lady, one that needs to get back home." He picked me up, and arranged for a lift to our house. I was extremely embarrassed, all I wanted to do was choose my adventure for the day.

It was just a few days later, that various contractors were called to the house for estimates on painting, remodeling and plumbing, the Bonzos were to become deep in thought about color schemes, and various changes they wanted to make. I certainly wanted to make a change, how about letting me wander where I want, down the lonely road for example, that would be a start.

Delivery trucks and packages kept arriving, with items purchased for the new house, so much so, the UPS driver became so familiar with me he actually knew my name. The mail person also calls me by name, since most often she has to drive right up to the house, with an arrnful of packages and catalogs, too much for the mailbox. All these parcels meant one thing, a lot of boxes to dispense with, seemingly Mr. Bonzo's forte.

The trash collector arrives each Wednesday, and so it was on the appointed day a few weeks later, that he hailed Mr. Bonzo who was busy inspecting his new toy in the driveway, a garden tractor, with "Hey there."

124

"Hello" he replied.

"You have an awful lot of trash" said the collector.

"Well, I have never seen beautiful trash" he responded.

"No, what I meant was, you have a lot of trash, how many people live here?" he inquired.

"Just two of us, and our dog" said Mr. Bonzo.

"I've never seen so much trash for two people" he said with a perplexed look on his face.

"Well, we've just moved here from California, two hundred boxes unpacked" he said proudly, and with a straight face added "Most of it the dog's."

The collector unimpressed muttered something to himself, and entered his truck, but as the weeks and months rolled by his muttering became louder and louder. Even now he still does the same thing, sometimes you can hear him from the house, and no doubt at the end of the lonely road.

Since the Bonzos discovered neighbors usually put out one can of garbage, the Bonzos have at least four, accompanied by several garbage bags without cans, an untold number of boxes, the result of those arrivals bought from the hundreds of catalogs addressed to Mrs. Bonzo and delivered by the mail person (who knows my name), which end up in the trash. It's a tribute to recycling.

As I once more lay on the, not as clean as it once was, kitchen floor, I couldn't help thinking while they finally made their choice of the new color scheme, I hope they choose a wheaten color so I blend in, but when not consulted, left to my own devices it can be a lonely road.

Chapter 31

THE TRACTOR

I was summoned to assemble on the driveway, outside the garage for the big event. You would have thought there was going to be a parade, or world peace had been declared, at the very least a marching band would be blasting off, I sat down next to Mrs. Bonzo with much anticipation.

It was official launch day for the tractor's maiden voyage, aboard, in the drivers seat, Farmer Bonzo. It was delivered from the local store, parked in the garage facing the door and it came with an instruction manual, something he does not consult whatever the product unless in dire need. This day was one of those days.

With a bottle of cheap champagne in hand, Mrs. Bonzo's role in the proceedings was to commission the vehicle with a swing of the bottle across the rear end. Regretfully she missed that, having swung the bottle on more than one occasion in the direction of her sweet lips. However she managed to let fly in the direction of the rear of Mr. Bonzo's head, hitting the target admirably, upon which he pronounced "Gentlemen start your engines" and did so, inadvertently put it in reverse and careered into the back of the garage, methodically rolling over several boxes marked fragile, still unopened from moving day draped with very small strips of scotch tape from packing. I never moved a muscle even though somewhat amused.

Undeterred, wearing, an old sweatshirt, long baggy khaki shorts, a bow tie and his pith helmet, which must have softened the blow from the bottle, he stormed forward this time, narrowly missing the fragile boxes, straight through the garage door, which thank goodness was open. He purchased this tractor in part, because

126

of the larger engine, fine wide cutting blades, and in the colors of his favorite soccer team, but it was engine size that dominated the launch. After whizzing across the driveway, over the grass through raspberry bushes and toward the electric fence their farming neighbors had put up, to prevent cattle roaming on Bonzo land, the tractor gathered downhill momentum, at an unrelenting pace, seemingly prepared for a NASCAR event, disappearing in the distance.

Mrs. Bonzo looked at me, bottle in hand and not for the first time she and I were in accord... will we ever see him again.

The fence not designed to hold back mad tractor drivers, caved easily as he passed between bewildered cows, who on hearing the sound of a racing throttle embarked upon a mild stampede to return to their barn at our neighbors farm, he continued unabashed toward the pond. It should be noted not one blade of grass was mowed up to this point.

While Mrs. Bonzo had the advantage of sipping champagne, I had no such distraction, I just couldn't keep my eyes off the whole spectacle, and frankly I didn't want to, since this was the most interesting moment for me since moving to Maine.

On the downward slope toward the pond lay a series of fir trees, pleasantly green and primed for Xmas distribution, they did however lay in the path of the runaway tractor. In the distance we could see Mr. Bonzo pulling different levers on the tractor, and at the same time attempting to correct the course of the vehicle. Having not read the manual he had no idea which lever did what, so although managing to avoid the trees, he started up the forty two inch blades, while meandering all over prime cow feeding grass, cutting it down to nothing. I guess the cows were going to have a surprise if they ever returned after this fiasco, not to mention the gentlemanly farmer whose land was cut to ribbons.

Mrs. Bonzo and I decided we had enough of Farmer Bonzo's antics, and despite his plight we returned into the house, as I ran in, faint chuckling could be heard from her, as she followed. Moments later we could hear the tractor returning across the driveway and into the garage. Surprisingly Mr. Bonzo was not at all flustered, as his muddy boots made their entrance on to the clean kitchen floor.

"What in the world were you doing? Asked Mrs. Bonzo as she finished the last of the champagne.

"Just giving it a test drive" he muttered softly, "No problem, I'm ready to mow the grass" he added.

I was ready to curl up in a corner somewhere, Mrs. Bonzo was ready for a nap, Farmer Bonzo on the other hand was ready to cut pastures new. Among the many accessories he purchased with the tractor was a spreader which according to that manual, if ever read, can be used to fertilize and spread seeds, and Mr. Bonzo's mission was exactly that. My mission was to remain in a lying position as if I was in a sleep mode, but I couldn't help wondering what tragedy would befell the local farming community if he really did fertilize something.

Once again we heard the tractor depart, I couldn't imagine what trouble he would get himself into next, but just as I was about to slumber, I was aroused by the crack of falling trees. Mrs. Bonzo also awoke, and we both rushed outside to see several birch trees at the back of the house laying horizontal, on the furrows and divots that was once prime meadow. Mr. Bonzo was not to be seen, although faintly one could hear the sound of the tractor in the distance.

On his eventual return some hours later, calls had to be made to tree fellers, and a tractor repair man to repair the damage to the blades, inflicted by the nutty tractor driver. Days later after loggers and the tractor had been towed away, Mr. Bonzo proudly announced he likes country life, and mowing grass was to become his new found passion. To this day it's a miracle the barn is still standing, and no more trees have fallen. Cows did return to their pasture, fresh grass aplenty, pleasantly motionless, although wary of oncoming traffic, I vowed to ignore tractors and mad Englishman, Mrs. Bonzo declared she will never be a farmer or ever clean the kitchen floor again.

After years of elegant dining, sophisticated soirees, shopping trips for designer clothing, now unbelievably drinking cheap champagne, and in particularly living in this part of the country, I wondered... What on earth was it, to this remote part of Maine, that could attract her.

Chapter 32

MELLOW YELLOW

Fall in all its glory, came and went. The Bonzos spent much of the time admiring the golden leaves and fall colors that people travel miles to see, and were so splendid in our own back yard.

I spent much of the time watching contractors tear off layers of wallpaper, that had accumulated over decades, and now would be replaced by the color scheme of Mrs. Bonzo, the old house would be revived afresh. When one morning a painter arrived with the curious name of Bugsy Peacorn, I just knew this would be fodder for my memoirs.

I have always greeted people at the front door, from puppy days in California, to now, with the fondest of jumps up their legs, and tail wagging, Bugsy was to be no exception, and got the treatment. I felt a certain reticence on his part, as I am sure the reader is aware, we Wheatons can sense reticence even if we can't spell it. Bugsy seemed ill at ease and I made no attempt to comfort him.

At the same time four cords of wood were being delivered, to fuel the ancient wood furnace in the cellar, and to be cut for the old Franklin fireplace in the living room, enough for the winter, and they were uncerernoniously dumped behind the garage. It was going to be Mr. Bonzos job to carry the logs to the cellar, a place I call 'Below stairs.' It's not a place I have ever been in to, or want to go to, and I have no desire to change my views on that.

"How are you going to carry all that wood into the cellar" asked Mrs. Bonzo addressing her husband. "You're not exactly bristling with muscles" she added.

"Don't know yet, but I'll think of something" replied Mr. Bonzo.

Bugsy whilst perched on a step ladder, splattered with a fair dose of paint on his head and shoulders, and rolling some of it on a kitchen wall, butted in with "I think I know who can help you."

"Who" said Mr. Bonzo as he too was splattered with a dose of very light yellow paint entitled "Jaune Ictere" according to the color chart they used to make their selection. Bugsy had turned round a little too hastily, with his roller still in his hand, and some paint made its way in Mr. Bonzos' direction.

"Lucien and Roget" he replied. "You can find them in town, although I must warn you, they are hard to cornmunicate with, since they speak a mixture of French and English, and they have trouble pronouncing words, and frankly I think they are not exactly all there in the head if you know what I mean.

Perfect for Mr. Bonzo I said to myself.

"I'll look them up" said Mr. Bonzo wiping off some yellow paint from his glasses, and muttering to himself something about needing windshield wipers.

As I have stated earlier, Mr. Bonzo considers himself something of a linguist, Mrs. Bonzo knows better since most of the time he doesn't even understand what she says, so much for Mr. Bonzo's International flair. There was the time he read a menu in French at a restaurant in Provence and proudly boasted of his ability to communicate Mrs. Bonzo's wishes for dinner. After letting the waiter know, in his best French, as to their choices they were somewhat surprised to be served pigs trotters in a snail sauce, instead of what they thought was going to be grilled sole. After much confusion, and a distinctly unpleasant meeting with the chef, he ended up with an omelet that night.

After searching frantically for a place to have me groomed not long after we arrived in Maine, they did find a place in a small town across the border in Canada, and every time we go there Mrs. Bonzo and I cover our ears as he insists on speaking French to everyone, even with the Customs Officer as we cross the International Bridge, I am surprised he hasn't been arrested, and that I am able to get a bath and be groomed to wheaten standards, but I think that's because they speak English both at the point of entry to Canada and at the grooming facility, and they generally take no notice of what he says in whatever language.

It was therefore not going to be a revelation, that he would try to find Lucien and Roget in town, and set off mentally thinking in French. In this part of Maine known as the St. Johns Valley, much of the population speak what is known as Arcadian French derived in part from slang, and nothing like that which is spoken in France. Mr. Bonzo didn't know that, and frankly I am not sure that would make any difference, to him.

Meanwhile back at the house under Mrs. Bonzo's watchful eye, Bugsy Peacorn was still busy redefining his paint application.

Since everyone in town knows everyone else, it wasn't difficult for Mr. Bonzo to find the two brothers, when he inquired about their whereabouts.

Most people suggested they might like to look elsewhere for help, since they had a reputation for being a little soft in the head, but Mr. Bonzo was undeterred.

"Just go the house next to the Shell station, and Lucien will be sitting outside" the townsfolk told him, and sure enough there he was.

Mr. Bonzo approached the slightly built middle aged man, sitting on a lawn chair, waving to traffic as it passed.

"Are you Lucien" asked Mr. Bonzo.

"Yeah up" came the reply.

"I'm Mr. Bonzo, and I need some help carrying cords of wood, to my cellar, could you and your brother Roget do that.

"Yeah up" Lucien said again, and then with something of a frown on his face added "Jaune jaune."

"How about tomorrow, say about this time, and you will tell Roget?" Mr. Bonzo went on.

"Yeah up" was the reply.

Mr. Bonzo departed after the short conversation secure in the knowledge he had accomplished his task, and returned to the house, whereupon entering he was not really surprised to see Mrs. Bonzo with yellow paint on her face, rather like fans who paint themselves in support of their team at a football game.

"Mission accomplished" he declared, Although I must admit it was a short conversation, and Lucien kept muttering something about yeah up and jaune jaune.

"Jaune is the French word for yellow" interrupted Bugsy, that's probably because you have yellow paint all over your face" inter rupted Bugsy, "I wonder why that is?" scowled Mr. Bonzo.

The next day Mr. Bonzo departed to pick up his helpers, carefully avoiding Bugsy on his way out, secure in the thought that he had removed all traces of jaune jaune, as he and Mrs. Bonzo had spent most of the day and night wiping off their faces with tur pentine, and they still reeked with its odor. I fortuitously remained unscathed, like missing the hit of a custard pie in a slapstick comedy, ...well almost.

Roget, a slightly larger man than his brother spoke some English, generally mixing both languages together in one sen tence, as did most of the population ofthe St. Johns Valley but this still proved difficult to understand in communication. On their return, Mr. Bonzo had a short meeting with them by the side of the pile of wood, explaining the task at hand. From the house Mrs. Bonzo, Bugsy and I could see him gesticulating, waving his arms and pointing to the house.

Mr. Bonzo opened with "We'll load the wood on my tractor cart, I'll drive to the back door of the cellar, then unload it.

Lucien's: "Yeah up."

Roget: Do ewe 'ave Ictere Jaune?

Mr. Bonzo: Pardon.

Lucien: Jaune jaune!

Bugsy now seeing the possibility of a conversation about to become heated, stepped into the fray, with the intent of translating, accompanied by Mrs. Bonzo and me, all of us with dabs of yellow paint on our faces.

"Sacre bleu, Lucien, zees personnes all have ictere jaune" said Roget.

"Yeah up" added Lucien, "Jaune jaune."

"No, no" said Bugsy, "Its yellow paint, not yellow jaundice" explaining in Arcadian French. Ictere being the French and Arcadian word for jaundice.

"How did they get that?" inquired Roget.

"I'd rather not say" retorted Bugsy.

With the misunderstanding resolved, they set about loading wood on Mr. Bonzo's tractor cart, I disappeared from view as did Mrs. Bonzo, after witnessing his first tractor outing. Bugsy was left out there staring at the three of them, paint roller in hand, using it as if he was a traffic cop, as they went back and forth. On a later inspection two trees had yellow paint marks on them, that would normally signify their removal, but divine intervention from Mrs. Bonzo saved them.

After many hours of loading and unloading, Mr. Bonzo the tractor driver, speeding from point to point, the brothers heavy with sweat from carrying four cords of wood, they entered the house, where Mrs. Bonzo was preparing lunch for everyone, and Bugsy was limping slightly having fallen off his ladder for the third time.

During the meal Lucien and Roget related as best they could, how they had lived in the Valley all their lives, never been anywhere else. Bugsy and others in the community had told the Bonzos, that a lot of people stayed away from them, thinking they were not quite right in the head.

Really were very sweet people, and obviously misunderstood, and like the Bonzos I took a great liking to them, and felt so much compassion for their situation. How sad it must have been, all their lives, to be a in a world where you can't communicate as you would like to with others, and they can't with you.

I sat down, looked at them with a tear in my eye, and reflected I think I know how you feel... If only I could tell them.